Death and Beyond in the Eastern Perspective

東方的死觀

Death and Beyond in the Eastern Perspective

A study based on
the *Bardo Thödol* and the *I Ching*

Jung Young Lee

AN INTER*f*ACE BOOK

An INTERFACE book, published by Gordon and Breach, New York

Copyright © 1974 by

Gordon and Breach, Science Publishers, Inc.
1 Park Avenue
New York, N.Y. 10016

Editorial office for the United Kingdom

Gordon and Breach, Science Publishers Ltd.
42 William IV Street
London W.C.2.

Editorial office for France

Gordon & Breach
7-9 rue Emile Dubois
Paris 75014

Printed in Great Britain by
Biddles Ltd Guildford Surrey

Dedicated to
Gy, Sue and Jong

ACKNOWLEDGMENTS

The author is indebted to the following for permission to reprint copyright materials:

Oxford University Press for permission to reprint from *The Tibetan Book of the Dead*, Compiled and Edited by W. Y. Evans-Wentz, 1960; Princeton University Press for permission to reprint from THE COLLECTED WORKS OF C. G. JUNG, ed. by G. Adler, M. Fordham, W. McGuire, and H. Read, tr. by R. F. C. Hull, Bollingen Series XX, vol. 11, *Psychology and Religion: West and East*, "Psychological Commentary on 'The Tibetan Book of the Dead' " (©1958 by Bollingen Foundation and ©1969 by Princeton University Press); George Allen & Unwin Ltd and Barnes & Noble for permission to reprint from *Eastern Wisdom and Western Thought* by P. J. Saher, 1969.

Preface

This is an attempt to explain the existential meaning and process of dying, death, after-death state, and reincarnation in the (classical) Eastern perspective. Perhaps it is necessary to clarify what is meant by the term "Eastern perspective" (in this book). It means the certain perspective or orientation which represents a more fundamentally Eastern than Western outlook. Since an absolute distinction between the Eastern and Western orientation is not possible, the term "Eastern perspective" is used here in a relative sense. One of the basic orientations which distinguish the Eastern from Western perspective is the way of thinking, which is the foundation of all other cognitive processes. It is the basic assumption of this book that the dominant tendency of the Western people is to think in terms of the exclusive method, that is, to make an "either-or" classification. On the other hand, the main trend of the Eastern people is to think in terms of the inclusive method, that is, to make a "both-and" classification. That is, perhaps, why one of *Newsweek's* editors commented on the difference between American and Chinese just prior to President Nixon's visit to China.

Where an American thinks in terms of "I", a Chinese is apt to think of "we". Where Western logic tends toward the absolutes of either/or, Chinese reasoning is based on the more harmonious blend of both/and. [1]

Since the Western people think more in terms of the absolute category of either/or, we can call it a Western perspective. On the other hand, the Eastern logic is more in terms of the inclusive category of both/and, so we can call it an Eastern perspective. Thus, the basic characteristic of the Eastern perspective is the inclusive way of thinking in all things. Since this kind of thinking is clearly expressed in the yin-yang relationship, it is often called the "Yin-Yang" way of thinking. [2] The purpose of the present book is then to study death and beyond in terms of this inclusive "yin-yang" way of thinking, which presupposes the world of change and relativity. That is why it should be differentiated from the Eastern concept of Death and Beyond, which draws sources from Eastern traditions alone. However, a study in Eastern perspective does not have to confine itself to Eastern traditions. It, therefore, attempts to integrate various existing insights of both Eastern and

Western traditions into a meaningful understanding of death and beyond from the most inclusive perspective, which is more fundamentally an Eastern than a Western outlook.

As to the representatives of Eastern perspective, two books, the *Bardo Thödol*, or the Tibetan Book of the Dead, and the *I Ching*, or the Book of Change, are selected. The former is to be understood as the study of death par excellence, and the latter as the standard work of metaphysics in Eastern perspective. Justifications for the selection of these two outstanding works have been provided in the first chapter. Since this work is primarily the correlation of these two books, it is principally directed to those who are interested in them, as well as those who seriously question the existential reality of death and beyond.

"Death is Birth and Birth is Death: The Parascientific Understanding of Death and Birth," which was written for *Systematics* (March, 1972), is reprinted in the third chapter with a slight alteration. My thanks are due to The Institute for the Comparative Study of History, Philosophy, and the Sciences for permission to reprint the article in this book.

In preparing this book I am deeply indebted to the encouragement and advice of Professor Ervin Laszlo, editor of the series: "Current Topics of Contemporary Thought", who made specific criticisms and suggestions to improve the book. I am grateful to Dr. Austin Kutscher, of Columbia University, who has kindly consented to write the Foreword to this book. Thanks are due to Dr. Edward A. Burtt, Dr. Wing-tist Chan, Dr. Hellmut Wilhelm, Dr. Herbert V. Guenther, and others who have directly or indirectly contributed toward the completion of this book. My special thanks are due to Stacey L. Edgar and Jill Gidmark, who have done an excellent job in getting the manuscript ready for printing. I am also indebted to the University of North Dakota for the Faculty Research Grant which made it possible to complete this book.

J.Y.L.

NOTES AND REFERENCES

[1] See under the title, "What It Means to Be Chinese," in *Newsweek*, February 21, 1972, p. 37.
[2] Cf. J. Y. Lee, "Yin-Yang Way of Thinking" in *International Review of Mission*, Vol. LX, no. 239, July 1971, pp. 363-370; J. Y. Lee, *The Principle of Changes: Understanding the I Ching* (New York: University Books, 1971), pp. 300 ff.

Foreword

Although a conceptualization of the word "thanatology" was described in detail early in this century by an eminent physician, Dr. Roswell Park, the default of the medical profession relegated the study of dying and death to the meditations of philosophy. There was scant, if any, cross-fertilization between academic philosophy and the clinical sciences until recent years. By modern definition, thanatology embodies the concerns of those dedicated to caring for the physiological, psychological and pathologic conditions of the human body, and the clinician finds himself reaching out from these confines to the philosopher for ethical and moral guidance. Such is the nature of an age where the technology of the scientist threatens to outstrip his morality.

Contemporary studies of dying and death have confronted a barrier constructed by the taboos and superstitions of the general public and the psychological denial of those engaged in the health professions whose great crusade is directed toward the defeat of death. Yet a start is being made to breach this barrier. Lines of communication are being stretched between the allied health sciences and those disciplines which formulate, enrich and preserve the intellectual heritage, the humanitarianism and the philosophical dimensions of modern culture — both Western and Eastern.

Goals are being set by interdisciplinary scholars and scientists as they study the ways for individuals to face and accept dying and death with maximum dignity. Likewise, ways are being explored so that guidelines may be offered the bereaved to help them accept the loss of loved ones and, in due course, through the work of grief, recover from the emotional impact of their bereavement. Medical specialists, social workers, the clergy, psychologists, nurses and others who deal with the cruel phenomena of diseases, human suffering, of living, and of dying are beginning the search for an accommodation between life as a reality and life as an ideal. Philosophers have preserved, interpreted and reinterpreted the messages of other centuries and other cultures to add a wisdom which is not limited by external factors nor restricted by institutional fiat. The clinician operates in a world fettered by the complexities of human relationships, disease, techniques, time and emotions; the philosopher is given freedom and has the opportunity to

ix

encompass and surmount these obstacles as he labors to create order in man's thought processes and activities.

To follow the path described in Professor Lee's exposition of the *I Ching* and *The Tibetan Book of the Dead* would be to extend new ethical values derived from ancient learning into the theoretical sciences, the practical sciences and the clinical sciences of today. Only man, among all creatures, is weighed down by the knowledge of his own mortality, yet he is blessed as the possessor of an intellect capable of expressing the dilemmas that this knowledge imposes. He is also the only creature able to achieve solutions for many of the problems of his life. But the fact of his mortality must still be faced and accepted; it cannot be solved or changed.

Professor Lee's interpretation of the philosophy of the East introduces into Western thought new guidelines by which each man can live in comfort with the thought of his own personal extinction. If Western thought cannot accept completely the inclusive perspective of the East which sees death as a part of life, perhaps it can, at the very least, make some attempt at integrating into itself ethical values and concepts which can serve to enrich its own concepts and widen the dimensions of its own perspectives on living and dying.

Within the discipline of thanatology (in reality a subspecialty of medical science) with its sharing community of many interreacting disciplines, of which philosophy stands well in the foreground, the creation of an atmosphere for the cross-fertilization of thought and the interaction between each discipline can result in greater dignity for the body of man and more profound wisdom for the minds of men.

Dr. Austin H. Kutscher
President, The Foundation of Thanatology

Table of Contents

I | Introduction

We live in a world civilization, in which both East and West are not apart. Scientific technology almost forces us to see ourselves as the citizens of the world. The electronic mass communication can instantly relay us news from all over the world. The supersonic air-transportation of our time creates in us the image that distance is no longer the real problem in understanding between the East and the West. Computer technology can assist us to detect almost all events in detail around the world. The moon is no longer the object of poetic romance; it came into the domain of technical civilization of our time. We begin to talk about the global village. The world is now seen as the colony of the earth in the vast universe. Even though this world-consciousness emerges out of the present predicament, we are still ignorant in the most profound area of our life. Our soul-searching question on the problem of death has never evolved much further than the primitive thoughts of our ancestors. As the world progresses toward the higher civilization, we must make an effort to study this ultimate quest of life and death. As we pursue the higher form of civilization and the broader knowledge of human issues, we seem to become more and more uneasy in discussing death in public. Dr. Belgum, professor of religion, University of Iowa, said, "Now sex is openly discussed and dying is obscene."[1] Death becomes a forbidden topic as life becomes precious. This is one of the greatest problems with which the Western civilization has failed to deal. The topic of death must not give the feeling of depression and uneasiness. People are often afraid to mention the word 'death'. Dr. H. H. Price, Professor Emeritus, University of Oxford, said,

Nowadays the subject of life after death is not merely a depressing one. It is something worse. It is a topic which arouses such strong and uncomfortable emotions that we prefer not to mention it at all.[2]

Death is certainly not only neglected but a taboo topic in America and in Europe. Because of this negative attitude, as Saher remarked, the problem of death is

not investigated properly in the West for fear of upsetting some long-held dogma, or else to avoid coming in conflict with a world-affirming optimism.[3]

1

Perhaps it is our immaturity to avoid consciously the reality of death, because we do not want to die even if it is unavoidable. We often behave like teen-age boys who don't want to know the reality of their girl friends, because they are afraid that they cannot keep the illusion of their love if they know the reality of those whom they love. It is the sign of our immaturity to avoid the real issue for the sake of superficial happiness. Death is a real problem which we cannot avoid. Why is this topic forbidden in the West? Why has this topic been neglected more in the West than in the East? [4]

There must be many different reasons why the West has failed to take the topic of death as seriously as has the East. However, one of the most important factors which has promoted the unhealthy attitude toward death is the dualistic value orientation in the West. The absolute dichotomy between good and evil may go back even to Zoroastrianism in Persia. This conflicting dualism between good and evil has been the dominant tendency of the Western thought. The Judaeo-Christian idea of creation and salvation has been interpreted by this dualism. Death is thought to be a result of man's sin (Genesis 3:3). Thus death has been closely associated with evil. And life is thought to be the gift of God, who is the source of goodness. Greek philosophy has contributed much toward the development of a conflicting dualism in the West. Particularly Aristotelian logic, the foundation of the Western way of thinking in the past, is the basis of an "either-or" way of thinking. It is the method of absolute categorization of things to either *this* or *that*. This kind of thinking has been the main characteristic of the West. In such thinking, death and life are in conflict, because both of them cannot exist together. We must choose *either* life *or* death. If there is none other than the "either-or" choice, no one may desire to take death. That is perhaps why life became the central affirmation of all values, while death became the ultimate negation of them. Since all value systems are centered on life, death means the deficiency of all values established in life. Death becomes the end of meaning and existence. Thus, we in the West stress the greater value in youth and health. In interviewing the old and dying patients in the hospital, the interviewer often hears a typical expression like this: "Do you really want to talk to an old and dying woman? You are young and healthy!" To be old and unhealthy means to be less valuable in society. Thus the old people in the West have been much neglected and isolated from the main stream of civilization. It is certainly a frightening and horrible experience to be old in this kind of society, where the value of dying is excluded from that of life. Therefore, the either-or way of thinking in the West is primarily responsible for this civilization, where life alone is valued and death is completely devalued.

The main thread of Western philosophy has been based on the exclusive way of thinking. As Saher said,

In Western philosophy an idea is *not accepted* unless proved to be correct. In the Eastern philosophy an idea is *not rejected* unless proved to be false. The attitude of Western philosophy is . . . what is *not proved* is to be treated as false. The attitude of Eastern philosophy is . . . what is *not proved* may be accepted as true until proved to be false. [6]

Western philosophy as a whole has been much preoccupied with sharp distinctions and analyses as the basis of proof because of the either-or way of thinking. As Professor Conger said,

Historically the West has been most concerned to introduce sharp distinctions of A and not-A.[7]

This A versus not-A type of thinking, that is, the either-or way of thinking, according to Saher, develops quickly into the bigotry of "not-A is identical with anti-A."

So that in our own day we hear such hysterical cries as "whoever is not against communism is for it," or "whoever is not baptized is an enemy of Christianity" and the like. [8]

Because of this kind of exclusive way of thinking in the West, what is intellectual is necessarily dualistic. [9] This is precisely why Western philosophy in general seems to fail to deal with the totality of human existence, which includes both life and death. It is certain that the either-or way of thinking, which presupposes the conflicting dualism, has created an unhealthy attitude toward death. Moreover, the validity of this kind of thinking is also questioned by the development of the new nuclear physics. Especially, in view of both Planck's quantum theory and Einstein's theory of relativity, the either-or logic is almost untenable. [10] Therefore, the failure of this kind of exclusive thinking, which is the Western perspective, may lead us to see the possibilities of understanding the more comprehensive view of life and death in Eastern perspective.

In contrast to the either-or way of thinking in the West, the Eastern people as a whole have been primarily interested in the integration of knowledge rather than the distinction within it. The main characteristic of Eastern wisdom can be its inclusiveness, while that of Western thought is its exclusiveness. The inclusive way of thinking in the East is expressed in the category of a "both-and" rather than an "either-or." The "both-and" way of thinking is not based on the conflicting dualism but on the complementary dualism. *Both* life *and* death are mutually inclusive and complementary to make the rounded whole possible. Because of the inclusive way of thinking, Eastern wisdom stresses the wholeness of reality. That is why, as Saher said,

A comparison with Eastern wisdom usually means a comparison of the *whole* of Western philosophy with only a *part* of Eastern philosophy. Eastern wisdom, like an iceberg, keeps the greater part of itself immersed and invisible. [11]

Because of this inclusive approach to the reality of human existence, the dominant trend of Eastern wisdom has been deeply concerned with the problem of both life and death. Certainly the problem of death has never been taken lightly in the East. Death becomes important because of life, and life is meaningful because of death. In this way both death and life are complementing each other. Thus the old in the East are not neglected but are still respected and cared for by society. To be old is in fact more valuable, because the values one accumulated in life can be retained even in one's death. Thus death does not destroy any value. Rather death makes values more valuable. In this kind of approach to life and death, the topic of death is fully discussed and investigated without any feeling of shame and depression. Since death has been accepted as a part of life, the inclusive way of thinking that is also Eastern perspctive can make a profound contribution to the understanding of death. In order to investigate the meaning and process of death and beyond in Eastern perspective, let us take up the two distinctive works, the *Bardo Thödol* and the *I Ching*.[12] They are the representatives of the Eastern minds par excellence. The *Bardo Thödol*, one of the most authentic records on death, is the practical instruction to the dying as well as to the living. It is still used in Tibet as the manual of death. As Lama Anagarika Govinda said,

Although the *Bardo Thödol* is at the present time widely used in Tibet as a breviary, and read or recited on the occasion of death — for which reason it has been aptly called "The Tibetan Book of the Dead" — one should not forget that it was originally conceived to serve as a guide not only for the dying and the dead, but for the living as well.[13]

Thus it is not something past but is a part of living reality in the life of Tibetan people. As a typical Western scholar, Saher witnesses the authenticity of the *Bardo Thödol* not only from his own experiences but from a purely metaphysical point of view. He said,

I am convinced that the *Tibetan Book of the Dead (Bardo Thödol)* is an authentic record of the dying hour and of the post-mortal state. I myself have tested in involuntarily. Twice in my life I have been very close to death and have had experiences which agree with the accounts given in the *Tibetal Book of the Dead.*[14]

This is certainly a personal testimony which is not easily dismissed. For Saher the *Bardo Thödol* also represents the outcome of pure metaphysical work and science:

The *Tibetan Book of the Dead* is the first record we have of a *purely philosophical* attempt at a coldly scientific, reasoned analysis of the after-death state uncontaminated by guess work.[15]

The above statement conveys his strong conviction as to the authenticity of the *Bardo Thödol* as a philosophical and scientific attempt at understanding death in the East.

Since the *Bardo Thödol* is written as a manual or a practical guide for the dying and the living, it does not deal with the metaphysical aspects of death.

We need a background knowledge to understand the profound implications of the *Bardo Thödol*. As the work which contains the metaphysical system of the practical instructions of the *Bardo Thödol*' the *I Ching* is selected because of its comprehensiveness as a metaphysical system in Eastern perspective. The *I Ching* is then selected here to complement the *Bardo Thödol*. The significance of the *I Ching* is clearly demonstrated in its historical influence on the Far Eastern people in the past. It is certainly unknown when this book was written, even though many different speculations have been made on the authorship. [16] However, it is one of the earliest works of Chinese minds. It represents the *ethos* of the Chinese people and the basis for their intellectual revivals in the past. It became the center of the "Hundreds of Schools" movement during the Han dynasty and the "Neo-Confucian movement" during the Sung dynasty. It was not only accepted by the Confucianists as their classical work but also by the Taoists. The *I Ching* has been the foundation of metaphysical systems in China, Korea, and Japan in the past. As Carl Jung said,

This work (The *I Ching*) embodies, as perhaps no other, the spirit of Chinese culture, for the best minds of China have collaborated upon it and contributed to it for thousands of years. Despite its fabulous age, it has never grown old, but still lives and operates, at least for those who understand its meaning. [17]

Since the *I Ching* represents the excellent minds of the Chinese people, it is selected to supplement the metaphysical background of the *Bardo Thödol*. By correlating these two books we may be able to represent not only the finest traditions of the East but the greater understanding of truth about death in Eastern perspective.

First of all, both the *Bardo Thödol* and the *I Ching* denounce any deterministic approach to reality. They do not say what is going to happen. They do not forecast what will take place. That is why they are not based on the causality principle. They are based on the synchronistic principle, which is an acausal connecting principle. Many occult literatures and divinations attempt to describe the future events in detail, but these two books do not forecast any facts or provide any proofs. After demonstrating the reliability of the *I Ching*, Carl Jung concluded:

The *I Ching* does not offer itself with proofs and results; it does not vaunt itself, nor is it easy to approach. Like a part of nature, it waits until it is discovered. It offers neither facts nor power, but for lovers of self-knowledge, of wisdom — if there be such — it seems to be the right book! [18]

Since everyone is different, having different problems at different moments of time, there is no way to forecast any facts or proofs, which can be applicable to all. Each of us has to find our own answer in respect to our own experience. The *Bardo Thödol* approaches the problem in the same way as does the *I Ching*. As Saher said,

It [the *Bardo Thödol*] does not pretend to forecast what will happen after death, but, should anything happen, it explains what it *cannot* be otherwise than. For instance, no one can forecast *what* a person will dream tonight, but one can say that whatever he may dream it will consist of seeing, hearing, or feeling, something and therefore will not be independent of imaginary sense of impressions.[19]

What Saher attempts to say is not really different from what Jung said about the *I Ching*. In both cases any deterministic approach is denounced. Thus, their approach is indeterministic because of the acausal connecting principle or the synchronistic principle. The characteristic of this indeterministic approach is in its inclusiveness.

The meaningful correlation between the *Bardo Thödol* and the *I Ching* is also possible because they presuppose the world of constant change and transformation. Within this changing world phenomenon, life and death are no exception to change.

This transciency of human life is a typically oriental thought found everywhere in Eastern writings from the *Rubaiyat* of Omar Khayyam to the *I Ching* in China.[20]

The title of the *I Ching* suggests that the change is the ultimate reality. '*I*' signifies change and '*Ching*', classic or book. Thus the *I Ching* means simply the book about the change. The Great Commentary to the *I Ching* said,

The Great Primal Beginning is found in the change. The change generates the two primary forces. The two primary forces generate the four symbols, which in turn generate the eight trigrams.[21]

It is the change which changes and moves all things in the universe. Things are produced and reproduced by the activity of the change. The same idea is also implied in the *Bardo Thödol*. It is the change which changes not only the life of man but also the dead. In other words, the phenomenology of death in the *Bardo Thödol* presupposes that the change is active in the consciousness of the dead. Without this kind of presupposition the *Bardo Thödol* is not effective. Saher was right when he said,

This [*Bardo Thödol*] single masterpiece of Eastern wisdom attempts to deal with the problem of changes in consciousness which takes place shortly before, during, and immediately after death.[22]

Both the conscious and the unconscious are within the realm of change. Nothing is possible without change, for the change is the ultimate reality. That is why one of the first initiators of the Neo-Confucian movement, Chou Tun-yi, said

If we investigate into the cycle of things, we shall understand the concepts of life and death. Great is the change! In it lies its excellence.[23]

The change transforms all things. It changes not only the body but the soul of man. In other words, this process of change is not interrupted by death. As Chuang Tzu said,

Truly is it said, "For the wise man life is conformity to the motions of Heaven, death is but part of the common law of change. At rest, he shows the secret powers of yin; at work, he shows the rocking of the waves of yang." [24]

The principle of change is the basis for our understanding of the phenomena of life and death. Both life and death are counterparts in the process of change. They are as Chuang Tzu said, macrocosmic symbols of yin and yang. Just as yin and yang, life and death are mutually interacting. The constant interplay of these two is the background of our understanding of the *Bardo Thödol*.

Since the process of change consists of the two opposite poles, that is, yin and yang, in everything there are these opposites, because everything is changing. These opposites are essentially undifferentiated, even though they are existentially differentiated. In other words, they are the same in essence but different in existence. Thus, they are essentially in a continuum. This essential continuum of the opposites makes the complementary dualism possible. In this continuum, the opposites are not in conflict but complementary to each other. In this kind of complementary relationship all things are essentially described in terms of a "both-and" category, which is a denial of the absolute dualism based on the Aristotelian logic of an "either-or" classification. As Carl Jung observes, the *Bardo Thödol*, like the *I Ching*, presupposes the "both-and" way of thinking:

The background of this unusual book (*Bardo Thödol*) is not the niggardly European "either-or", but a magnificently affirmative "both-and". [25]

This inclusive way of thinking, that is, the "both-and" or "yin-yang" way of thinking, is the characteristic of the Eastern wisdom. [26] Both the *I Ching* and the *Bardo Thödol* share this magnificently affirmative category of "both-and", which differentiates them from the absolute category of "either-or", which is the characteristic of the Western way of thinking.

Finally, there is a meaningful correlation between the concept of the Tao in the *I Ching* and the Clear Light of the Void in the *Bardo Thödol*. The Tao in the *I Ching* is expressed in terms of the change itself, which is also changeless. The change changes all things but the change itself is changeless. Thus the paradoxical definition "The change that is changeless" has been the persistent claim of many commentators on the *I Ching*. [27] The Tao is none other than the change that is changeless. Thus, Chu Chai says, "The word *I* (change) is used interchangeably with *Tao*." [28] If we look at the Chinese word for Tao, it is easy to notice this paradoxical statement. The Tao means the Way, which in its original form consists of a head, and then the character for "going" or "moving along", and underneath, the character for "standing still", which is omitted in the later way of writing. [29] From the analysis of this word "Tao" in Chinese character, the ultimate is both changing and unchanging at the same time. Thus the concept of the Tao corresponds to the idea of change itself, which is also changeless. In the *Bardo Thödol* the ultimate reality, which corresponds to the Tao or change itself in the *I Ching*, is known as the Clear Light of the Void, the *Dharma-Kāya*. The Clear Light of the Void is the Essential Body of Buddha, which is beyond form and beyond discrimination and differentiation. It is the Light itself, the source of all lights and colors. It is formless, which means colorless. It is the void of colors but the source of all colors. Thus it is similar to the Tao, the source of all changes, which is also formless and nameless. [30] Both the Tao and the *Dharma-Kāya* transcend the distinction between the poles of opposites. Both the form and formlessness as well as the change and changelessness are one and are in the undifferentiated continuum.

As a result we see the possibility of combining both the *Bardo Thödol* and the *I Ching* for our investigation into the phenomena of death in Eastern perspective. The former is explicit in the phenomenology of death, while the latter is implicit in it. Without the former the latter is unable to understand the actual phenomena of death. Without the latter the former is incapable of discerning its profound implication. Thus we need both of them to understand the full implications and phenomena of death. The *I Ching* is necessary as the background of the *Bardo Thödol*. Through the use of these two excellent works of the East in a complementary manner, we may be able to find a key to the mystery of dying, the post-mortal state, the process of reincarnation, and various forms of change taking place on the other side of life.

NOTES AND REFERENCES

[1] *The New York Times*, March 28, 1971.

[2] His address appeared in *Religious Studies*, Vol. III (1968), pp. 447-459.

[3] P. J. Saher, *Eastern Wisdom and Western Thought* (London: George Allen and Unwin, 1969), p. 255.

[4] However, I must recognize that there is a growing awareness of this problem in recent times. For example, the recent formation of the Foundation of Thanatology in New York is one of the significant movements toward this awareness.

[5] Kübler-Ross, *On Death and Dying* (New York: Macmillan, 1969), p. 22.

[6] Saher, *op. cit.*, pp. 204-205.

[7] See his "Radhakrishnan's World" in *Library of Living Philosophers*, Vol. VIII, p. 111.

[8] Saher, *op. cit.*, p. 252.

[9] Chang Chung-yuan, *Creativity and Taoism: A Study of Chinese Philosophy, Art, and Poetry* (New York: Julian Press, 1963), p. 103.

[10] Jean Gebser, "Foreword", in Saher, *op. cit.*, p. 10.

[11] Saher, *op. cit.*, p. 210.

[12] *I Ching* has been translated into English by James Legge (Oxford University Press), Richard Wilhelm (Princeton University Press), and others.

[13] See his "Introductory Foreword" to *The Tibetan Book of the Dead*, compiled and edited by W. Y. Evans-Wentz (Oxford: Oxford University Press, 1960), p. lix.

[14]. J. Saher, *Eastern Wisdom and Western Thought: A Comparative Study in the Modern Philosophy of Religion* (London: George Allen and Unwin, 1969), p. 148.

[15] *Ibid.*, p. 248.

[16] See J. Y. Lee, "Some Reflections on the Authorship of the *I Ching*," in *Numen: International Review for the History of Religions*, Vol. XVII, Fasc. 3, December 1970, pp. 200-210.

[17] Carl G. Jung, "In Memory of Richard Wilhelm," delivered in Munich, May 10, 1930. It is reprinted in Appendix, *The Secret of the Golden Flower* (New York: Harcourt, Brace and World, 1962). Trans. by R. Wilhelm. See p. 140 of this book.

[18] C. Jung, "Foreword" in the Richard Wilhelm's translation, p. xxxix.

[19] Saher, *op. cit.*, p. 248.

[20] Saher, *op. cit.*, p. 280.

[21] *Ta Chuan*, Sec. I, Chap. 11.

[22] Saher, *op. cit.*, p. 116.

[23] Chou Tunyi, *An Explanation of the Diagram of the Great Ultimate* (from *T'ai-Chi-t-u shuo* in *Chou Lien-ch'i chi'i*, 1: 2b).

[24] See Arthur Waley, *Three Ways of Thought in Ancient China* (New York: Macmillan, 1939), pp. 44-45.

[25] C. Jung, "Pschological Commentary" in *The Tibetan Book of the Dead, op. cit.*, p. xxxvii.

[26] See J. Y. Lee, "Yin-Yang Way of Thinking," in *International Review of Mission*, Vol. LX, no. 239, pp. 363-370.

[27] See Hellmut Wilhelm, *Change: Eight Lectures on the I Ching* (New York: The Bollingen Foundation, 1960), p. 23; J. Y. Lee, *The Principle of Changes, op. cit.*, p. 89.

[28] Ch'u Chai, "Introduction," in the *I Ching* (New York: University Books, 1964), p. xc.

[29] See the pictogram of *Tao*, 道 , which is the combination of 首 , head, and 辶 (辵), moving.

[30] *Tao Te Ching*, Chap. 1 and 32.

2 | *Death is in Life and Life is in Death*

The meaning of death is commonly misunderstood in our time. Death is often seen in separation from life. Death is something strange to life. In fact death is regarded as the ultimate enemy of life. We have done everything to fight back the power of death. Perhaps, the power underlying the civilization of our time can be attributed to our desire for survival. Darwin's theory of evolution is precisely based on this power of survival. Our fundamental urge is seen in terms of our defense against the power of this ultimate enemy of life. It becomes the fundamental motive for the improvement of our life and society. Our technical science is the tool of expanding life-power against death. We joined ourselves with pieces of machines to extend our power to live. We in technical civilizations have amputated the inanimate machines from our toes to hairs to expand our life. For the expanding of our life-power, we have not only attempted to prolong our lives but to intensify our lives through technical devices of our time. Medical science is interested in prolonging human life through the incorporation of artificial or alien organs and substances in the body. The communication technology expanded the sight of life through the vast media system. The technology of transportation has expanded the space of our lives through the intensified speed. Everything that our technology attempts to do in our civilization is a fight against the deadly power of death. Civilization as a whole is fundamentally the human reaction to the power of death. Even religious teaching attempts to react against the power of death. The strength of religion is to give life to the dying and the dead. That is why the idea of resurrection became the focal point of the Christian faith. Resurrection became the symbol of fulfilling this fundamental urge of man to live or to live again. It is used as the symbol of counteraction against the power of death. Thus Paul said, through the resurrection of Christ, "Death is swallowed up in victory." (Cor. 15:54.) It is the Christ who conquered the last enemy or the ultimate enemy, that is, death. Death is not only the enemy of man but also of God, because God was in Christ to reconcile the world to Himself. In this sense the Hellenistic Christianity saw death as the ultimate enemy of life. That is perhaps why death has become a forbidden topic to discuss in our time. Death is

10

a taboo topic because of its inherent evil. We have attempted to eliminate death from life, but our technology has failed to do so. Thus what we can do now is to dismiss its existence from life. This is a superficial way to treat death, but this is only possible in the light of the life-affirming and death-negating civilization of our time. Our kind of superficial approach to death does not solve any problems of death. Rather it intensifies it and mystifies its reality. Why do we have to think that death is the enemy of life?

It is my persistent theme that the misunderstanding that death is the enemy of life comes from the above way of thinking. Our way of thinking, particularly in the West, has been dominated by the conflicting dualism. This kind of dualism presupposes the ultimate dichotomies between good and evil, light and dark, or between life and death. The conflict-dualistic thinking has been nurtured and taught through the use of Aristotelian logic "either-or" classification. It is the logic of the "Excluded Middle", because the validity of the middle between the two extremities of "either-or" is excluded from this kind of thinking. It is the absolute classification of things without allowing the possibility of relativistic qualities. Thus it is one-sided thinking, because one extreme has to be denied to assert the other. In other words, in this "either-or" way of thinking, to assert the validity of one is to deny the validity of the other. Let us apply this kind of thinking to the idea of death and life. In the "either-or" way of thinking we can *either* accept the reality of life *or* the reality of death, and to accept that of death means to deny that of life altogether. If we think life deals with good, death must then deal with evil. Since this kind of thinking became the seedbed of scientific technology in the West, the scientific way of thinking stresses preciseness through discrimination and analysis rather than comprehensiveness through inclusiveness and totality. The real trouble with the "either-or" way of thinking in relation to death and life, as well as to all other ultimate matters, is the tendency to absolutize relative phenomena.

An Eastern perspective on life and death is quite different from the "either-or" way of thinking. It is a noumenal approach to phenomena, rather than a phenomenal approach to noumena. A noumenal approach to phenomena presupposes that the reality is known in its wholeness and totality. Thus phenomena are seen within that totality of noumenon.[1] Thus it is an essential approach to existence. Existence, that is, phenomenal appearance, is always relative to essence, which is in a continuum. Thus the noumenal or essential approach is inclusive, because noumenon or essence is in a continuum. Thus an Eastern perspective to death and life denies any absolute and deterministic way of thinking. It is inclusive and indeterministic, because it makes use of the acausality principle or synchronicity, rather than the deterministic category of causality principle. That is why the Eastern point of view tends to make use of the "both-and" way of thinking to describe the phenomena of life and death. If we use this way of thinking in describing the phenomena of death and life, we ought to say that *both* death *and* life are one and inseparable from the noumenal point of view. In other words, from the noumenon or the essential continuum, both life and death or yang and yin are undifferentiated, even though they are two different forms of existence from the phenomenal point of view. Thus, from the noumenal point of view, that is, from Eastern perspective, life and death are one, just as yin and yang are one, for they are undifferentiated. Death is then only the phenomenal distinction of life, and life is also the phenomenal distinction of death. One cannot exist without the other, just as yang cannot exist without yin and yin without yang. There is no way to separate death from life, because the former cannot exist without the latter. It is impossible to think of death without thinking of life, because both of them are inseparable in any circumstance. That is why if there is no life, there is no death; if there is no death, there is no life. That is precisely why Chuang Tzu said, "Where there is life, there is death; and where there is death there is life."[2] This intrinsic unity and oneness between death and life makes it possible to say that death is in life and life is also in death at the same time. Both death and life are essentially one but existentially two. Thus from the Eastern approach, that is, the essential point of view, death is in life and life is in death simultaneously. How can it be? Can it be varied if death is the opposite of life and life is the opposite of death?

It is almost nonsensical to say that the opposites are the same. Since life is the opposite of death, to say life is in death means to unite the two opposites. It is a paradoxical statement for those who think in terms of the "either-or" logic, which is the Western perspective. However, it is not a paradox at all if we think in terms of the "both-and" way of the Eastern perspective. The "both-and" way of thinking is based on the relationship between yin and yang, which is the primordial category of all existence. The yin-yang relationship is representative of the sub-microcosmic to the macrocosmic realities. For example, in the sub-microcosmic category the yin-yang may represent the positive-negative energies in nuclear structures. In the macrocosmic structure the yin-yang represents the earth and heaven or *K'un* and *Ch'ien*, the first two hexagrams in the *I Ching*. When they are related to human existence, they represent his death and life. Yin represents death, and yang represents life. Just as life and death are opposite, yin and yang are opposite in existential characters. Therefore, let us examine how yin is in yang and yang is also in yin, in order to illustrate death is in life and life is also in death at the same time.

In order to demonstrate that yin is yang and yang is also yin, let us see the *T'ai Chi T'u* or the Diagram of the Grerat Ultimate, which expresses the best in our understanding of yin and yang relationship.[3] This Diagram is seen all over China, Korea, and Japan in temples, pieces of art work, window design, and many other places. This Diagram of the Great Ultimate is the symbol of the Korean flag. If you have not seen the diagram, you can easily draw the symbol. Take a circle and divide it into two equal parts by drawing an S-shaped curve from top to bottom. One part of the circle should be dark and the other light. A light dot is to be placed in the centre of the dark and a dark dot in that of the light. Here, we have attained a perfect symmetrical symbol of the change in which both yin, or dark and yang, or light, are mutually intertwined together in harmony. The diagram attempts to illustrate that

light is not absolutely light but is also dark, because the dark dot is in it. Dark is not absolutely dark, because a light dot is in it. Just as the light principle presupposes the existence of the dark, the dark principle also presupposes the existence of the light. Since dark principle is yin and light principle is yang here, we can also say yin presupposes yang, and yang presupposes yin at the same time. In the light the dark is hidden, and in the dark the light is hidden. Thus the change changes either from dark to light or from light to dark. When the dark dot in the light principle increases, the light begins to decrease; and when the light increases, the dark begins to decrease. In other words, one is relative to the other. When one grows, the other decays; and when one decays, the other grows.

It is more clearly expressed in the symbols of line in the *I Ching*. Each hexagram in the *I Ching* consists of six lines of either the divided or the undivided. In the hexagram the line can change either from the divided to the undivided or from the undivided to the divided. The divided line represents yin principle, and the undivided line represents yang principle. Thus yin line (— —) always changes to yang line (———) by merging together. At the same time the yang line (———) always changes to yin line (— —) by separation. What makes yang different from yin is a certain state of existence in which the line is not divided. What makes yin different from yang is also a certain moment of existence in which the line is broken. Since the union and separation of line are constantly in process without ceasing because of the change, the differentiation between yin and yang is only the existential moment of change. However, it is also important that the moment of yin is never in separation from that of yang in any sense, because yin or the divided presupposes yang or the undivided. Since the divided line (—— ——) or yin is possible because of the undivided line (————) and the undivided because of the divided, we cannot even talk of one without the other. Since one presupposes the existence of other, we cannot speak of yang without yin and yin without yang. Thus to speak of yang is to speak of yin and to speak of yin is to speak of yang at the same time. However, when we speak of yang, yang is revealed to our mind; and when we speak of yin, yin is revealed to us. When yang is revealed to us, yin is hidden as the background of yang; and when yin is revealed to us, yang is hidden as the background of yin. Thus yang is yin manifested and yin is yang unmanifested. If we apply this kind of relationship to life and death, we can easily conceive that life is death manifested and death is life unmanifested. Life is the foreground of death, and death is the background of life. Thus, they are mutually inclusive and inseparable at any circumstance. Here, the original statement that life is in death and death is also in life is restated in terms of their background and foreground. However, we may still question the reality of the yin-yang relationship, which the *I Ching* describes. If the relationship is acceptable in our experience, we do not see any reason to reject the idea that death is in life (unmanifested) and life is in death (manifested). Thus let us attempt to see the relevance of the yin-yang relationship to our experience.

The yin-yang relationship in the change, according to the Great Commentary to the *I Ching*, comes from the observation of natural process in the universe. As it is said,

The holy sages surveyed all the possible rules of changes and movements under heaven. They contemplated the forms and phenomena, and made the representations of them, which were summarized in the symbols (of *yin* and *yang*). [4]

Since the symbols and their relationship are taken from the process of nature, it is proper for us to see the relevance of their relation to our experience in nature. The words of yin and yang were originally grown out of the southern and northern slopes of mountains. They are primarily the symbols of light (yang), because of the sun on the southern slopes, and of dark (yin), because of the shade on the northern slopes of mountains. Using the original meaning of yang and yin, or the light and dark principles, we may be able to see their relationship to our daily experience. Light and dark are opposite in phenomenal appearance. They are considered to be the opposite poles, yet they must be one and identical in essence. To illustrate it let us consider our everyday experience of the light of the day and darkness of night. One day consists of both the light and dark. Thus let us think of a day in terms of its wholeness, that is, both the light and dark parts of day together. When the sun is at the zenith, light is intensified at its maximum. When light is in its fullest manifestation, we fail to notice the existence of darkness within the light. How many of us really recognize the existence of dark in the shining and bright midday! We do not see the dark element in the bright sunshine, because we have been taught to think in terms of an "either-or" classification.

If we think in terms of the "both-and" way, we can easily conceive both light and dark at the same time. The bright midday is none other than the greatest intensification of light as well as the greatest de-intensification of darkness. On the other hand, the dark midnight is none other than the greatest intensification of dark power and the greatest de-intensification of light. Thus the real difference between day and night is none other than the difference in intensity between light and darkness. Both the midday and the midnight represent the extreme poles of these two powers. Within these poles they change from their minimum to their maximum intensities. As soon as one reaches its maximum, it starts to retreat toward its minimum. When it reaches its minimum, it again grows toward its maximum. Everything changes in this pattern of growth and decay or intensification and de-intensification. When light is at its maximum, it begins to lose its intensity and finally becomes its minimum. On the other hand, darkness grows as light decreases and it reaches its fullest intensity at midnight. As soon as dark reaches its maximum, it starts to yield its power to light. Thus light cannot exist without dark, and darkness cannot exist without light. The light is light because of the darkness, and the dark is dark because of light. They are mutually interdependent. Darkness is none other than light unmanifested, and light is darkness manifested to us. In other words, yin is yang unmanifested, and yang is yin manifested. Thus, we can also say life is death manifested, and death is life unmanifested. Just as darkness is the background of light and light the foreground of darkness, death is the background of life and life is the foreground of death. They are mutually interdependent and interrelated, because they are essentially undifferentiated.

Perhaps, one of the best illustrations to explain the yin-yang relationship in our experience is the relationship between silence and sound. Silence corresponds to yin and sound to yang. Just as yin is the background of yang, silence is the background of sound. We hear the sound of music, but we do not hear the silence behind it. However, when the sound of music stops, we hear silence revealed to us instantly. Those who think in terms of the "either-or" way of classification often think that silence and sound are two separate entities. But, those who are oriented toward the Eastern perspective think in terms of the "both-and" way. For them *both* silence *and* sound are inseparable. Silence is none other than the sound unmanifested, and sound is the silence manifested to them. They are one, but manifest in two different phenomena. Anyone who is trained in music can notice that sound is none other than silence vibrated. On the other hand, silence is none other than the sound unvibrated. They appear to be different but they are essentially the same. Just as the two poles of silence and sound are one, death and life are one from the inclusive point of view, that is, the essential approach to phenomena.

Let me take some obvious examples to explain the yin-yang relationship further. We begin to see that the contemporary scientific research helps us to see the shortcomings of the "either-or" way of thinking, which has been in the minds of the Western people since the formulation of Aristotelian logic. One of its shortcomings is closely related to the unbreakable law of nature, that is, the conservation of energy. According to this law, energy can neither be created nor destroyed but only transformed from one form to the other. Where does this energy come from? It is based on the energy-mass equivalence formula, $e = mc^2$, which derived from the special theory of relativity. According to this formula, we see the continuity between e, or energy, and m, or mass, in a certain condition, which is expressed in c^2 or the speed of light. In other words, energy is in mass and mass is in energy as long as a certain existential condition is provided. They are not separate but one in two different manifestations. Energy is none other than mass unmanifested, and mass is none other than energy manifested. Let us suppose that mass represents yang and energy represents yin. Here, yang is none other than yin or energy unmanifested, and yin is none other than yang or mass manifested in our visible forms.

Another important clue which gives the possibility of "both-and" thinking is the validity of both the wave theory and the quantum theory of light. To claim the validity of both is in fact the denial of the validity of the "either-or" way of thinking. For those who are inclined to think in terms of an "either-or" way it is almost a paradoxical and non-rational case to accept both of them as valid. However, for those who are oriented toward the Eastern perspective, it is not a problem but the confirmation of their method of thinking. The radiation of energy in the forms of both continuity and discontinuity has to do with its existential manifestations. The light which appears in the form of waves is also the same light which appears in the form of quanta. The former represents continuity, while the latter discontinuity. The form of continuity is expressed in the symbol of yang, the undivided line (————). On the other hand, the form of discontinuity is expressed in the symbol of yin, the divided line (——   ——) in the *I Ching*. The existential situation which unites the divided is called yang, and that which divides the united is called yin. To unite the divided is to presuppose the existence of the divided, that is yin (or the quantum theory). To divide the united is to presuppose the existence of the united, that is, yang (or the wave theory) as its background. Therefore, the wave theory presupposes the quantum theory of light, just as the latter presupposes the former. They are mutually interdependent to each other. One cannot separate from the other. Their relation, thus, confirms the yin-yang relationship.

Some of these illustrations help us to see that the Eastern perspective, which is based on the yin-yang relationship, is not only desirable but essential in our understanding of death in relation to life. Death is defined in terms of life, and life is understood in terms of death. To separate one from the other is in fact to dismiss them all together. That is why death cannot be the ultimate enemy of life. They ought not to contradict or conflict with each other in a real sense, but ought to complement and fulfill each other for the completion of the whole man. Thus, to separate death from life is to make life incomplete and meaningless.

I think Johnson's definition of death is much closer to the Eastern perspective on death. He said,

Death is to be explained in terms of life. It is a weak and indeed, insofar as it marks the final disintegration of one's *nephesh*, the weakest form of life; for it involves a complete scattering of one's vital power. [5]

Death as the weakest form of life also implies that life is the weakest form of death. Here, we see the continuity between life and death. The weakest form of life corresponds to the strongest form of death. The former represents the de-intensification of yang (or life power) to its minimum. On the other hand, yang represents the de-intensification of yin (or the power of death) to its minimum. Since the fullest de-intensification of yang means the fullest intensification of yin, the least or minimum form of life is identical with the maximum form of the other side, that is, death. Moreover, the fullest de-intensification of yin means the fullest intensification of yang. Thus the minimum form of death corresponds to the maximum form of life. The yang which has the creative power makes life possible. On the other hand, yin represents the responsive power, which is receptive to the life-giving power of yang. In this sense the least expression of yang or vital power is identical with death. Johnson elucidates this idea a little further:

At death a man's vital power (yang) is found to be broken up in disorder, its unity shattered; and the result is that as an individual he drags on in a relatively weak existence, which is as opposed to life in its fullness as darkness is to light. [6]

Leshan also agrees with the idea that both death and life share the same vitality. He said,

The viewpoint that has seemed to make the most sense to the writer is that life and death are both aspects of the same *vital* center, the same existence. [7]

This *vital* center is analogous with the change itself, which is also *Tao*, the inmost core of moving world. Therefore,

"Life" and "death" are human terms, and are meaningless from the standpoint of eternity (or *Tao*). [8]

They are one in essence. Death remains as the background of life for the living. But when he is dead, the power of death or yin becomes the foreground of life. At death the weakest form of life (or yang) will remain and the fullest manifestation of yin takes place. Thus Lao Tzu said,

Life leaves and death enters. Three and ten parts accompany life; three and ten parts accompany death. [9]

The thirteen pieces of body will remain whether man is dead or alive. Therefore no new pieces are created or destroyed by death. The only difference between life and death is the change or transformation of one to another existential form. Life and death are essentially the same, even though they appear to be quite different. In essence everything is in a continuum, the undifferentiated reality of noumenon, which is the matrix of yin and yang as well as death and life. That is why, as Kasternbaum said,

It has been suggested that life and death might be regarded as a continuum rather than as a dichotomy. [10]

Death does not take away life. Rather it weakens life, because life has weakened death. Death is the other side of life, just as life is the other side of death. Thus he who lives has experienced death. "Death is present in every life process from its beginning to its end." [11] To know how to live is to know how to die. Man lives to die, for death is the fulfillment of life. Man also dies for life, for life is born out of death. Without death there is no life, and without life there is no death either. Life and death are united to make the whole man possible. To separate death from life is to separate man's own existence. In his true self both death and life meet and become the undifferentiated whole. Thus it is said,

Whatever is here, that is there; what is there, the same is here. He who seeth here as different, meeteth death after death. "By mind alone this is to be realized, and then there is no diffeence here. From death to death he goeth, who seeth as if there is difference here." [12]

NOTES AND REFERENCES

1 Dr. Saher is in agreement with me when he said, "Eastern wisdom is far more interested in the *noumenon*; whereas Western philosophy appears to be far more interested in phenomenon." See P. J. Saher, *Eastern Wisdom and Western Thought* (London: George Allen and Unwin, 1969), p. 208.

2 *Chuang Tzu*, II. 2.

3 The Diagram of the Great Ultimate is found in Chou Tun-yi's (周敦頤) *Tai-chi-t'u shuo* (太極圖說).

4 *Ta Chuan*, Sec. I, Chap. 8.

5 Aubrey R. Johnson, *The Vitality of the Individual in the Thought of Ancient Israel*, 2nd ed. (Cardiff: University of Wales Press, 1964), p. 88.

6 *Ibid.*, pp. 94-95.

7 Lawrence Leshan, "Psychotherapy and the Dying Patient," *Death and Dying*. Ed. by Pearson (Cleveland and London: The Press of Case Western Reserve University, 1969), p. 30.

8 Donald Munro, *The Concept of Man in Early China* (Stanford: Stanford University Press, 1969), p. 128.

9 *Tao Te Chin*, Chap. 50.

10 Robert Kasternbaum, "Psychological Death," in *Death and Dying op. cit.*, p. 23.

11 Paul Tillich, *Systematic Theology*, III, pp. 52-53.

12 *Katha Unpanishad*, IV, 10-11 (Swami Sharvananda's translation).

3 | *Death is in Birth and Birth is also in Death*

Just as death and life are inseparable, both death and birth are interdependent. Even though they are opposite in their appearance to us, they are not really differentiated in their essence. Thus when they are seen from the Eastern perspective, which is also the noumenal approach to phenomena, they are one and the same. Just as life is the other side of death, birth is none other than the other side of death. Death is then the background of birth, and birth is the foreground of death. Death is not possible without birth. Death is the end for the living but the beginning for the dead. Birth is the beginning for the living but the end for the dead. However, when death is seen from this side or the side of the living, it is the de-intensification of yang or the vital power of life. Birth, on the other hand, represents the intensification of yang. At the moment of death, yang is at its minimum intensity, which makes death the weakest form of yang or life. On the other hand, it is the moment when yin is at its greatest. At the moment of birth, yang is at its expansion from its minimum intensity to its maximum, while yin begins to decrease in intensity. Both death and birth begin at the same point, where the process of change takes place. Both of them also end at the same place, where the process of change takes place.

We start dying the moment we are born. The rate of metabolism in our bodies begins to slow down immediately after conception. Birth is the cause of death.[1]

And death is the cause of birth. In other words, what makes birth, makes death possible. It is the change which changes and transforms all things including birth and death. The change according to the *I Ching* is the ultimate, which transcends the category of our description. Thus every phenomenon is attributed to the change. "Death is only a change of forms."[2] Birth is also a change of forms. It is then the change which operates in all phenomenal appearances through its two arms, yin and yang.

Everything including birth and death has yin and yang, because everything is in the process of change. Nothing is possible without change. Since the change is responsible for all births and deaths, we cannot create or destroy anything. It is not the we who gives birth and death. However, we can make

20

use of the power of change for our own end. When a man is killed by a car accident, for example, he is the victim of the power of change, which has been misused by the driver of that car. When man dies through a cancer, for example, he is the victim of the change through the medium of a cancer. It is the nature of cancer to become one of the most effective media to transmit the power of change to make a radical change in man. Many medicines become the effective means to change in a counter-direction, that is towards life rather than towards death. Whatever we have done or created in the name of technology or God, in the final analysis, the change is responsible. When a baby is born, we must give a credit to the change for this new creation. However, this is not a new creation in a strict sense. It is none other than the renewal of the old through the process of change. The change renews constantly, just as it makes things old. Birth is the renewal of the old, while death is the degeneration of the new. The world is in constant change and transformation from the old to the new and from the new to the old because of the constant birth and death. Birth and death are necessary for change, for they are the opposite poles of changing process. In every complete cycle of change there are birth and death, the maximum intensity of yang and yin. Within these poles of death and birth a full cycle of change takes place. Some of the cycles are long and slow, but some others are short and fast in change. Each moves according to its unique components, which are none other than the various intensities of yin and yang interaction. Because each has different components and intensities of yin and yang interplay, no one is alike in the process of change. However, regardless of their way of change, all things which change have these two poles of birth and death. All the living animals and insects have these poles. Everything has them. Since every cycle of change has both death and birth, the great cycle of change which has many small cycles of change has many deaths and births. From birth to birth and from death to death all things are in the process of constant change and transformation. Our birth and death are among many deaths and births which have been going on indefinitely through the very presence of eternal change.

If death and birth are parts of changing process in the universe, we must not consider them unnatural. To die is a natural process of change, and to be born is the natural act of change also. Even though a baby can be created in a test tube, it is a product of change. If the change makes things natural, everything is natural because of the change in all things. Man often attempts to make natural unnatural. However, our birth and death can be more spontaneous if we let the power of change work in us. Spontaneity is an act of harmony, while constrained behaviour is the act of disharmony. Whenever our act is in disharmony with all other processes of change in nature, we often call it unnatural behavior. Whenever our act is harmonized with the process of change in nature, we call it natural behavior. That is why our feeling of guilt to the dying is none other than our failure to harmonize ourself with the natural process of change in the cosmos. Guilty feeling is the reflection of man upon the cosmic process of change, rather than his interaction with the person who is dying. Of course, we feel guilty immediately if we are part of that which causes him to die. From the phenomenological approach to the noumenon, the feeling of guilt is known in one's relation to others. However, from the noumenal approach to phenomena, that is, the approach of the *I Ching* on Eastern perspective to reality, the feeling of guilt is none other than one's failure to harmonize his change with the cosmic process of change. This disharmony comes from his constraint of the power of change for his own end. Thus, whenever man attempts to manipulate the power of change for himself, he gets this feeling of disharmony with his surroundings, which receives the immediate effect of his manipulation. I believe this kind of feeling is given to all creatures, because it is none other than the indication of his disharmony with the cosmic process of change. This indication, which is often called sin by religious groups, may help him to throw himself into the process of cosmic change or even restrain himself until he is forced to go through the radical change, which may even result in death. We get this kind of indication or guilty feeling when one of our intimate friends is dead. In the loss of someone close to us we get the sense of emptiness or absence. The feeling of guilt is created by this emptiness which disrupts the process of change. This kind of feeling is present when a piece of furniture is removed from a room. The removal of furniture may disrupt the balance of creative process in a home. Thus we often have the empty feeling, which is none other than the guilty feeling neutralized in space. The funeral rites, for example, have more than a mere implication to comfort the family and friends of the dead. They have important functions to restore the harmony of process of change. They have a profound implication to the cosmic reintegration in the process of change.

On the other hand, birth creates different kinds of feelings in the family. It is not the empty feeling but the added feeling or feeling of fulfillment, which is expressed in joy and happiness. Thus when a child is born in a family, the new situation is to be created. The feeling of fullness created by the birth of a new baby is an expression of space, which has an immediate effect upon the radical transformation of birth. This kind of feeling is created through the sudden outburst of yang or vital life-energy at birth. Because of this outburst the normal process of change is interrupted. Readjustment is needed to include the new expanding power of yang, which vitalizes the immediate surroundings. Thus, the birthday celebration ought to have the same implication as the funeral service, that is, to restore the normal function of change. Perhaps that is why in China the rites of birth are so closely related to the ancestor worship. In the *Li Chi* (Book of Rites) both marriage and birth rites were to "secure the service in the ancestoral temple." [3] Even though birth is taken quite differently from death, they are not really different from the point of view of the whole. Death and birth are relative to the process of change. Thus the process of change as a whole does not alter. As we said, birth and death are the change of forms in different directions. Birth means the expansion of yang, which also means the contraction of yin at the same time. Death means the expansion of yin and contraction of yang at the same time. Thus, when they are seen from the undivided whole or the continuum of change, which includes both yin and yang, they are one in two different directions of movement. We also see that the feelings of fullness and emptiness are complementary to each other. Thus the difference between death and birth is only phenomenal. In essence they are one and the same when they are seen from the totality. They are different because of a certain direction of manifestations. In other words, birth is the reverse side of death, and death is also the other side of birth. Lama Govinda said it well. He said,

What we call birth is merely the reverse side of death, like one of the two sides of a coin, or like a door which we call "entrance" from outside and "exit" from inside of a room! [4]

Perhaps the door is a good metaphor to illustrate the relationship between birth and death. It is a door which can be opened both ways. When it is opened from inside the room toward the outside, it is similar to the process of death. On the other hand, when it is opened toward the inside, it is analogous to the process of birth. The only difference between them is the direction of opening. In other words, the difference between birth and death from Eastern perspective, that is, the point of view of the "both-and" way, is the difference in directions. From this illustration, we can say that death is birth outwardly directed and birth is death inwardly directed.

The problem of using the metaphor of the door to illustrate the process of birth and death is its concept of space. The idea of going out and coming in, or exit and entrance, can create a conceptual problem in the organic view of the world. However, the metaphors of the conscious and unconscious in relation to the process of birth and death seem to be more feasible than the opening and closing of the door. They are favorite symbols of Carl Jung in describing the relationship between life and death. The disadvantage of using these metaphors, of course, as Carl Jung himself testified, is the Western understanding of their psychological implication. As Jung said,

Whenever the Westerners hear the word psychological, it always sounds to him like *only* psychological. [5]

However, as Jung intended for the metaphors to be inclusive enough to include the whole self, I am willing to use the conscious and the unconscious to imply the meaning of yang and yin as expressed in the *I Ching*.

If we use the *conscious* and the *unconscious* to include all the qualifications which make a whole person, we may be able to carry out our task successfully. Using the metaphors of the *conscious* and the *unconscious* as more than a mere psychic aspect of a person, that is, to use them to represent the whole self, we may be able to define the relationship between death and birth. The phenomena of death and birth are none other than those of the *conscious* and the *unconscious* of man. Death implies the minimum *conscious* with the maximum *unconscious* expansion. On the other hand, birth implies the maximum expansion of the *conscious* and the minimum expansion of the *unconscious*. Since the *conscious* and the *unconscious* are essentially in a continuum, where one can be transformed into the other, they are complementary to each other. In this kind of complementary relationship we can easily say that death is birth more *unconscious* in process, and birth is death more *conscious* in process. Thus the real difference between death and birth is intensity in direction. Death is more intensively *unconscious*, while birth is more intensively *conscious*. The former moves towards the deeper unconscious realm of human existence, while the latter moves towards the higher conscious realm of human nature. However, when the *unconscious* reaches to its utmost degree of intensity, it begins to yield itself to the *conscious*. Thus death is the process which continues from the domination of the *unconscious* over the *conscious* to the maximum expansion of the *unconscious*. In the *Bardo Thödol* it is described as the *Chikhai Bardo*, the first stage of death, which is clearly differentiated from the following two stages of *Chönyid* and *Sidpa Bardo*. The *Chikhai Bardo* is the most crucial period of death stages. The last two stages of *Bardo* are to be understood as the life of death.[6] On the other hand, birth is the process which continues from the domination of the *conscious* over the *unconscious* to the maximum expansion of the *conscious*. It may correspond to a period from the time before birth to full recovery of the *conscious* after birth. Dr. Dubler-Ross explains it well. She says,

It [dying process] is a gradually increasing need to extend the hours of sleep very similar to that of the newborn child but in reverse order.[7]

The process of birth and death is the same except its direction which is completely opposite. What makes death really different from birth is none other than the direction of movement. The counter-movement of birth and death is quite clearly expressed in the *I Ching*.

In the *I Ching* there are 64 hexagrams, which represent the germinal or archetypal situations of the universe.[8] Even though each hexagram is autonomous in itself, it is also related to other hexagrams. It is both independent and interdependent at the same time. It consists of 6 lines of either broken or unbroken lines to signify yin and yang forces. If we observe the hexagrams carefully, the real difference between birth and death is none other than the direction of movements. Let us begin with the 24th hexagram or the *Fu* (復), which means the Returning, or the beginning of renewal. It is the symbol of new beginning of yang force in the midst of yin domination. When it grows to its fullest or maximum degree, it is symbolized in the first hexagram, *Ch'ien* (乾) which means Heaven or the Creative power. Let me draw the hexagrams to illustrate the process of birth before taking up the process of death.

— —	— —	— —	— —	— —	———
— —	— —	— —	— —	———	———
— —	— —	— —	———	———	———
— —	— —	———	———	———	———
— —	———	———	———	———	———
———	———	———	———	———	———

FU   LIN   T'AI TA CHUANG KUAI   CH'IEN

The above hexagrams can help us to visualize the combinations of yin and yang lines. The broken lines represent yin powers, and the unbroken lines represent yang powers. Let us take the hexagram *Fu*, which has only one yang line at the beginning (counts always from bottom up). It is the symbol of returning from the other side, the realm of death, which is symbolized by *K'un* or the Earth, the matrix of all yin principles. This hexagram represents the eleventh month, the month of cold winter (December-January). The symbol of this hexagram is thunder within the earth. It is the emergence of new life within the soil. It is only a germinal beginning, the very beginning of birth. Wilhelm's commentary is helpful to realize the meaning of this hexagram. He said:

In winter the life energy, symbolized by thunder, the Arousing, is still underground. Movement is just at its beginning; therefore it must be strengthened by rest, so that it will not be dissipated by being used prematurely. This principle, i.e., of allowing energy that is renewing itself to be reinforced by rest, applies to all similar situations. The return of health after illness, the return of understanding after an estrangement: everything must be treated tenderly and with care at the beginning, so that the return may lead to a flowering. [9]

It is then the sign of new life-energy emerging out of the yin-dominated region of death.

The hexagram *Lin* (臨) means "Approaching great" or "Becoming great". It consists of four yin lines and two yang lines on the first and second places. Because one more yang force is added to *Fu*, it signifies the movement toward the great becoming. It represents the twelfth month which corresponds to January-February. In this time the life-power slightly begins to advance toward the fuller growth. Thus, if we think of the hexagram *Fu* or Returning as the conception of a child, this hexagram represents the second or third month after conception. It is the time of movement toward growth.

The hexagram *T'ai* (泰) literally means "peace", which is the most perfect symbol of harmony between yin and yang forces. As we see from the symbol of hexagram, it consists of two trigrams: the trigram *Ch'ien* or Heaven below and the trigram *K'un* or Earth above. Since the former is light principle, that is, yang principle, it goes upward. The latter is the heavy principle or yin principle, so that it tends to come down. Therefore, both heaven and earth conspire with each other to produce all things. The Judgment of this hexagram says, "The great approaches and the little departs. It is a sign of progress and success." [10] This is the first month, which corresponds to February-March, at which time the life-power is well prepared for the new spring. It may correspond to the fourth or fifth month of development, the safest period of fetus.

The hexagram *Ta Chuang* (大壯) means the great power or becoming greatly powerful. As we see, the yang lines overcome the yin lines in number. There are four yang lines and two yin lines. Thus yin power is overshadowed by yang force. It is the beginning of the break-through. In other words, the yang power of life-energy is great enough to fulfill the meaning. It corresponds to the second month, that is, about March-April, at which time the sprouts are in full power to come out above the ground. At this time the fetus is grown to full strength.

The hexagram *Kuai* (夬) means the break-through. It finally breaks open. It signifies the very moment of birth. The baby is born. The long process of the waiting period is over. *Kuai* is then the symbol of birth. As it is said,

This hexagram signifies on the one hand a breakthrough after long accumulation of tension, as a swollen river breaks through its dikes, or in the manner of a cloudburst. [11]

The struggle to overcome the power of death is over. He is born! Thus it is linked with the third month, corresponding to April-May, at which time things burst out from the ground.

Birth becomes real when the child is fully recovered from the sudden break-through from the womb. Thus the hexagram *Ch'ien*, or the Heaven (also the Creative), ends the process of birth. As we see, it has all yang lines only. It is the fullest expansion of the vital life-energy. With this hexagram birth completes itself. It belongs to the first hexagram and the prime principle of yang forces. It is symbolized by the dragon, which represents the source of power and energy exceeding all other creatures. It is the fourth month, corresponding to May-June, when the light-giving power is at its zenith right before the summer. It is potency of unlimited power to expand and grow. Thus this is the good place to end the process of birth. As the process of birth ends, the reverse movement of death begins. However, this movement or the countermovement must be understood as a simultaneous action.

The process of death then begins with both the decrease of yang power and the increase of yin power at the same time. This kind of process is quite opposite to the process of birth. Thus we begin with the hexagram *Kou*(姤) and end with *K'un* (坤). It is the reverse movement or the other side of the process of birth. Let us draw the hexagrams again as we have done before to visualize their constituents of yin and yang lines.

```
─────  ─────  ─────  ─────  ─── ───  ─── ───
─────  ─────  ─────  ─── ───  ─── ───  ─── ───
─────  ─────  ─── ───  ─── ───  ─── ───  ─── ───
─────  ─── ───  ─── ───  ─── ───  ─── ───  ─── ───
─────  ─── ───  ─── ───  ─── ───  ─── ───  ─── ───
─── ───  ─────  ─────  ─────  ─── ───  ─── ───
```

 KOU   TUN   FOU   KUAN   PO   K'UN

As we see from the symbols of hexagrams, the yin movement begins with the hexagram *Kou*, which means what the symbol indicates, that is, the sudden confrontation of yin force in the midst of yang powers. Yin is the symbol of female as well as the dark principle, which leads to decay and death. No one wants to have this kind of attack by the bold and/or bad woman, as Legge says, in the midst of the active life. This is the reverse of the hexagram *Fu*, which gives the beginning of life-energy. Because of the bold appearance of yin or shadow in the midst of all yang and bright occasions, it is the beginning of death or the disintegration of yang power. The yin line at the beginning is more like the first confrontation of heart attack to a healthy young man. This sudden confrontation of the power of yin is the beginning of the process of death.

The hexagram *Tun* (遯) consists of two yin lines on the first and second places. It means retreat or withdrawal, which is the opposite of the approach symbolized by *Lin*. In other words, it is the other side of *Lin* or Approach. As Wilhelm said:

The power of the dark is ascending. The light retreats to security, so that the dark cannot encroach upon it. This retreat is a matter not of man's will but of natural law. 12

Man cannot do the changing process, which brings forth the power of yin. Man cannot avoid the coming death. He is destined to die. This is a natural law of change, not of his own volition. After the first heart attack, for example, he cannot resume his work as usual. He has to retreat or restrain himself in all things. It corresponds to the sixth month, that is, about July-August, at which time the forces of winter are already showing their influence. The power is at the yin side or evil side. Do not resist it. As Jesus said, "But I say to you, Do not resist one who is evil." (Matthew 5:39.)

The hexagram *Fou* or *P'i* (否) comes next. It corresponds to the hexagram *T'ai*, the peace and harmony of heaven and earth. Since *Fou* is the other side of *T'ai*, it means confusion and disorder or stagnation. It means the negative inclination to life. This time the image of heaven or *Ch'ien* is above and the image of earth or *K'un* is below. This is the reversal of the *T'ai* or peace. Since the *Ch'ien* is above, this means the Creative power is externalized. On the other hand, the Receptive power is internalized. Since the Receptive power or yin is the power of death, death got hold of him. The power of death has occupied the center of one's life. It corresponds to the seventh month, or August-September, at which time the process of growth stops. As Legge says:

Genial influences have done their work, the processes of growth are at an end. Henceforth increasing decay must be looked for. [13]

The hexagram *Kuan* (觀) is the reverse of the hexagram *Ta Chuang*. As we see from the diagram, it has four yin lines and two yang lines. Yin has the dominant force over yang powers. From its shape the name is adopted. It looks like the observation tower; thus, it is called the wide view, or contemplation. When we analyze the hexagram into two trigrams, we get the trigram *K'un* or the earth below, and the trigram *Sun* or wind above. Since it corresponds to the eighth month or September-October, it suggests the cold northern wind begins to prepare for the coming winter. It is the end of autumn followed by the initial signal of cold wind from the north. This is then the time of contemplation. Religion becomes important at this time of trouble. Thus the commentary to the Judgment says, "The ablution has been made, but not yet the offering." [14] I think this is the stage of one's preparation for the final death. There is no hope to overcome the powerful influence of yin. The power of death has already overcome the power of life. It is more like the fourth stage of dying process, in which the dying knows the coming death and is grieving for himself in painful depression.[15] As soon as this stage passes away, the final moment of death comes to him.

The hexagram *Po* (剝) is the reverse of the hexagram *Kuai* or the break-through. As we see from the image of the hexagram, it is the last stage of death. There is only one line of yang power, which retains his life. It is the very moment of death, or a dying hour, which is often called the fifth stage of death. The dying is no longer in struggle but accepts the fact of dying as inevitable. In this moment, the dying is no longer fighting back for life. He accepts death calmly without fear. As Kübler-Ross said,

It is as if the pain had gone, the struggle is over, and there comes a time for "the final rest before the long journey" as one patient phrased it. [16]

Thus this hexagram is called "disintegration" or "splitting apart". The *T'uan Chuan* or the Treatise on the Judgment says, "It is the cessation of normal process and looks in a sign." [17] Here, the sign which he looks for is that of death or the coming of the Great Light at the very moment of death. It is the time of disintegration of the body as well as the *consciousness*. Thus the *Tsa Kua*, or the Miscellaneous Remarks on the Hexagram, says, "*Po* means decay." As Wilhem said:

The dark lines are about to mount upward and overthrow the last firm, light line by exerting a disintegrating influence on it. The inferior, dark forces overcome what is superior and strong, not by direct means, but by undermining it gradually and imperceptibly, so that it finally collapses. [18]

It represents the ninth month, which corresponds to October-November. Winter has already come and the cold or yin is finally to overcome the warmth. Even though the hexagram *Po* as a whole is the image of a house being shattered and collapsed, there is an element of calm and steadiness in it. The image is the mountain resting on the earth. The trigram *Ken* (☶) is a symbol of steadiness, which occupies the place above that of *K'un* or earth (☷). Even at the last moment of one's death there is a calm and steady emotional rest. Thus,

At the end of it is often the dying who comfort the living. Even so self-centered a figure as Louis XIV said to those around his deathbed, "Why weep ye? Did you think I should live forever?" After a pause he reflected with equanimity, "I thought dying had been harder." [19]

This final stage of death is followed by *K'un*.

The hexagram *K'un* (坤) is the reverse of *Ch'ien* or the primal power of creativity. *K'un* or Earth is, as we see, the primal power of Responsivity or yin principles. It represents the complete conquest of death over life. It is the maximum expansion of yin power. Body returns to ashes and dust to earth. However, as soon as the disintegration takes place, there comes also the process of integration from its background, the power of *Ch'ien*. The process of disintegration is followed by the process of reintegration, because yin has in itself yang, which will grow as soon as yin decays. This power of reintegration, which comes from the very existence of yang power within yin just as yin is in yang, is known as the power of *karma*, which is a key to the process of reincarnation. The *K'un* or the Earth is not only the end of living but the source of all living. It is the mother of all, because it presupposes the existence of all creative power, *Ch'ien*. That is why the hexagram *K'un* is followed by the hexagram *Fu* or Returning. In this way another cycle of life and death begins again.

As we have seen from the diagrams, the movement of yin is the counterpart of that of yang. However, the process of their change was identical. Therefore, the real difference between the process of death and that of birth is only the direction of movement. Both the processes of death and birth take place simultaneously. Thus death is the other side of birth, and birth is the other side of death at the same time. The correlation of these two processes of death and birth has been affirmed by many doctors:

In arguing for an expanded notion of death, doctors also mention the characteristic return of the dying to infancy. Gradually they sleep longer each day, until they wake for only minutes at a time. Emotionally, the dying become increasingly dependent. Waking in the night they may cry if they discover they are alone, or sink back to sleep if someone is there.[20]

These descriptions show that the process of death corresponds to the process of birth. Modern experiments begin to see the profound implication of the *I Ching* in this matter.

We can then conclude that, from the point of view of the *I Ching*, death is birth outward-directed and birth is death inward-directed. Death and birth are one and inseparable. Thus, it is said, "What is within us is also without. What is without is also within." [21] The former is the background of the latter, and the latter is the foreground of the former, when they are seen from the point of view of the living. On the other hand, birth is the background of death, and death is the foreground of birth, when they are seen from the point of view of the dead. The *I Ching* attempts to see them, not from the side of the living only, but from both sides of the living and the dead together. Since death and birth are one and inseparable, we cannot say one without the other. If we accept the idea of the *conscious* and the *unconscious* as the representation of yang and yin in relation to the self of man, we can say birth is none other than death *conscious*, and death is birth *unconscious*. Since the *conscious* is in the *unconscious* and the *unconscious* is in the *conscious*, just as yang is in yin and yin in yang, we can say that the process of birth is within the process of death as well as the process of death within the process of birth. They are mutually inclusive and complementary. Thus from the noumenal point of view, that is, the Eastern approach to reality, death is in birth and birth is also in death. That is why Paul Tillich says, "The conditions of death are also the conditions of life." [22] Both death and life, as well as the process of death and birth, are simultaneously co-existing in the true Self, the noumenal reality. From this noumenal point of view, as Saher said, "Man does not exist in time, time exists in his consciousness." [23] Time does not change the change, but the change changes time as well as space. Both time and space are relative to the change, which changes all things. Thus, from the point of view of the *I Ching*, time and space cannot be separated in the process of both birth and death. Time is in the process of birth and death. In this respect, we say again death is not followed by birth or birth followed by death, but both death and birth are simultaneously taking place. Thus death is in birth and birth is in death. They are one of two different manifestations, for they are essentially undifferentiated in the continuum of changing process.

NOTES AND REFERENCES

[1] Edward Conze, *Buddhism: Its Essence and Development* (New York: Philosophical Library, 1951), pp. 23-24.

[2] P. J. Saher, *Eastern Wisdom and Western Thought* (London: George Allen and Unwin, 1969), p. 283.

[3] Quoted in Feng Yu-lan, *Chung-kuo Chieh-hsueh Shih* (Shanghai, Commercial Press, 1933), Vol. I, Trans. by D. Bodde, *A History of Chinese Philosophy* (Princeton University Press, 1952), Vol. I, p. 356.

[4] Anagorika Govinda, "Introductory Foreword" in *The Tibetan Book of the Dead*, Ed. by W. Y. Evans-Wentz (London: Oxford University Press, 1960), p. liii.

[5] Carl Jung, "Psychological Commentary" in *The Tibetan Book of the Dead*, p. xxxviii.

[6] Death here means the process of dying rather than the life after death.

[7] Elisabeth Kubler-Ross, *On Death and Dying* (New York: Macmillan, 1969), p. 99.

[8] For the comprehensive treatise on hexagrams and germinal situations see J. Y. Lee, *The Principle of Changes: Understanding the I Ching* (New Hyde Park: University Books, 1971).

[9] *The I Ching or Book of Changes: The Richard Wilhelm Translation*, rendered into English by Cary F. Baynes (3rd Ed., Princeton: Princeton University Press, 1967), p. 98.

[10] This is the translation of the original version: " 本小往大來詩 ."

[11] *The I Ching: The Richard Wilhelm Translation*, p. 166.

[12] *Ibid.*, p. 129.

[13] The *I Ching*, James Legge Translation (Oxford: Clarendon Press, 1899), p. 85.

[14] *The I Ching: The Richard Wilhelm Translation*.

[15] Elisabeth Kübler-Ross, *On Death and Dying* (New York: Macmillan, 1969), pp. 75ff.

[16] *Ibid.*, p. 100.

[17] The original text is as follows: " 順而止之觀象也 ."

[18] *The I Ching: The Richard Wilhelm Translation*, p. 93.

[19] Thomas Powers, "Learning to Die," in *Harper's Magazine*, June 1971, p. 80.

[20] Thomas Powers, *op. cit.*, p. 79.

[21] Katha Upanishad, II, iv, 10.

[22] Paul Tillich, *Systematic Theology*, Vol. III (Chicago: University of Chicago Press, 1963), pp. 54, 52-53.

[23] Saher, *op. cit.*, p. 117.

4 | The Spiritual Body and the Archetypes of Personality

One of the most crucial questions concerning life after death has to do with the existence of the spiritual body, or the counterpart of the physical body, which is also known by many different names such as the ethereal body, energy body, bio-plasmic body, and many others. If death means the complete extinction of everything which man has in himself in life, it is almost impossible to believe in the life after death. If there is an eternal life or rebirth as it has been taught by many religious traditions in the past, there must be some kind of individuation which sustains the existence of the self even after death. Without some kind of body or structural form it is difficult for us to conceive of any kind of possible life. Therefore, it is important to investigate the possibility of the existence of the spiritual body, or the counterpart of the physical body. Of course, it is not possible for us to prove or disprove its existence, but at least we can demonstrate certain propositions and evidence to support the possibility. In doing this we can apply the principle of change as clearly expressed in the *I Ching*.

The absolutistic category of an "either-or" way of thinking cannot demonstrate the possibility of the existence of the spiritual body, or the counterpart of the physical body. It has to claim the existence of *either* the physical *or* the spiritual body. It cannot accept both of them at the same time, since it cannot conceive of the reality of two counterparts as true. It is not, therefore, able to deal with the problem of the spiritual body.

However, reality in Eastern perspective, which is based on the principle of changes in the *I Ching*, makes use of the "both-and" way of thinking, because reality deals always with yin and yang. Since everything can be classified in terms of the yin and yang relationship, which is the primordial category of all existence, it is possible to presuppose the existence of both the physical and the spiritual body in terms of yin and yang symbols. Just as yang represents life and yin death, the physical body, which is closely associated

32

with life, is yang, and the spiritual body, which is closely associated with death, is yin. Just as yin and yang are counterparts, the spiritual body and the physical body are counterparts. Thus, the relationship between the spiritual body and physical body is relative to the relationship between yin and yang. Just as yin and yang are mutually inclusive and interdependent, both the spiritual body and the physical body are complementary to each other. Yin cannot exist without yang and yang without yin. Thus, if yin exists, yang must exist at the same time. If yang exists, yin must also exist simultaneously. Since the physical body exists, the spiritual body must exist, according to the yin-yang way of thinking. In other words, if we affirm the existence of the physical body, it means also the affirmation of the existence of the spiritual body at the same time. To deny the existence of the spiritual body, that is, the denial of yin, is in fact to deny the existence of the physical body, that is, the denial of yang. Perhaps, that is why Paul said, "If there is a physical body, there is also a spiritual body." [1] In the Upanishads, the inseparability of these two bodies or existences is depicted in the two birds clinging to the same tree (body).

Two birds, friends, always united, cling to the same tree [body]. One of them eats the sweet fruit of the *pippala* tree [the fruit of actions]; the other looks on without eating. [2]

One is active and the other is inactive. One corresponds to yang, and the other to yin. Both of them are united together.

The interdependence of both the spiritual body and the physical body makes us believe that the former alone cannot exist after death. If we believe that the physical body is completely disintegrated at death, it is not possible to believe that the spiritual body alone can exist without the physical body. Therefore, we must come back to the question of the physical body at death. Does the physical body really destroy itself when man is dead? We must answer this question if we are interested in the spiritual body.

This question forces us to think about the nature of the physical body more carefully. What do we mean by the physical body? What happens to it when man dies? If we mean by the physical body merely the sum of various tissues and chemical elements, we know that they are going to disintegrate at death and return to nature. However, the physical body is more than the sum of chemical substances. It includes the psychic and mental structures based on empirical experiences. Thus the physical body is the whole disposition of the empirical self. In this sense it is the sum of the qualities which constitute the form of life. The spiritual body also means more than a mere invisible substance. It signifies the total person who is the counterpart of the empirical self. Thus in both cases we mean the whole person. They are complete in themselves, but their completeness is conditioned by their interdependence. Just as yin and yang are complete yet different, both the spiritual body and the physical body are different but complete in themselves. That is why they are compared with the two birds clinging to the same tree. Perhaps it is also helpful to illustrate their relationship from Fan Chen, who says:

The spirit is the same as the body and the body is the same as the spirit. Therefore, when the body exists, the spirit exists, and when the body declines, the spirit is destroyed . . . The spirit to the concrete stuff is like sharpness is to the knife, and the body to the function is like the knife to the sharpness. The name of sharpness is not knife and the name of the knife is not sharpness. However, without sharpness, there will be no knife, and without knife, there will be no sharpness. [3]

The physical body is the foreground of the spiritual body, while the latter is the background of the former. In life the physical body is manifested in the spiritual body. In death the spiritual body manifests itself and the physical body is latent. Since the physical body is closely related to life, it is to be understood as the totality of the conscious self. On the other hand, the spiritual body, which is more closely related to death, is then the total structure of the unconscious self. Perhaps this kind of distinction is helpful in seeing the relationship between them.

In the relationship between death and life, Johnson's definition of death as "the weakest form of life" [4] is most helpful. To say death is the weakest form of life does not mean to deny the final disintegration of physical substances. Thus Tagore said, "We may die but not perish." [5] Death means the complete dissolution of physical entity into natural phenomena, but the body of the *conscious* seems to remain in the weakest form. According to the *Bardo Thödol*, the mental-content of the dead remains and is to be transformed into various forms of visions in the after-death state.

It asserts repeatedly that what the percipient on the *Bardo* plane sees is due entirely to his own mental-contents, that there are no visions of gods or of demons, of heavens or of hells, other than those born of the hallucinatory *karmic* thought-forms constituting his personality, which is an impermanent product arising from the thirst for existence and from the will to live and to believe. [6]

Since the dead experiences none other than the hallucinatory manifestations of his own mental-thought acquired in his empirical experience, there must be a form of the empirical consciousness which retains the mental-contents. The vivid description of the after-death state in the *Bardo Thödol* is based on this idea that the dead can retain his thought-form or the form of consciousness. If the form of the empirical consciousness is not destroyed by the disintegration of the physical entity at death, certainly death can be the weakest form of life because of this consciousness. This feeblest form of the *conscious*, which remains even after death, is the basis of the hope for the immortality of souls and the process of reincarnation. If there is no possibility of continuation between the *conscious* and the *unconscious* or between life and death, death is an extinction, not a radical form of transformation. Since death cannot be an extinction in a strict sense because of the law of conservation, there must be a radical transformation taking place at death. There is no doubt that there is a radical transition of mass into energy through the deformation of the bodily system at death. It is possible that the thought-form of *sangsāric* experience is retained in a certain energy form of the *conscious*. If the energy form of mental contents can be retained in a certain pattern of ideas or the *conscious*, we may be able to go along with Carl Jung on the idea of the archetypes of personality, which are eternally inherited forms and ideas without any specific content. As long as the visions the dead sees in the after-death state are reflections of his own *sangsāric* experience, there must be some kind of ethereal or spiritual form which can retain the experience. This kind of form or body which is not affected by death is the archetype, which maintains the *conscious* at its feeblest level even after death. Then it is the archetype which makes the continuation between death and life possible. The *conscious* is at its weakest at death, but the *unconscious* is at its strongest at death, because of the archetypes. Without presupposing the existence of archetypes, it is difficult to see death and life as a continuum. The relationship between the *conscious* and the *unconscious* of the archetypes at death can be illustrated in the hexagrams in the *I Ching*.

If we look at the hexagram 23 or *Po*, the symbol of the dying moment of life, it is depicted in terms of the mutual relationship between the *conscious* and the *unconscious*.[7] In this hexagram we see the feeblest form of yang lines on the top and the rest of them represent the strong powers of yin. Since yin is analogous with the *unconscious* and yang with the *conscious*, the former represents the strong *unconscious* and the latter the weakest form of the *conscious*. We see clearly from this hexagram that the *conscious* is at its weakest and *unconscious* is at its strongest at the moment of death. Both the *conscious* and the *unconscious* are relative to the hexagram, which is called the germinal situation or the archetype. From this hexagram or archetype we observe an interesting phenomenon in relation to the *conscious* and the *unconscious* or *yang* and *yin* lines. Since the archetypes are analogous to the hexagrams in the *I Ching*, every one of them consists of 6 lines of either yin or yang elements. Thus the delimitation of archetypal forms to a definite quantity helps us to see proportional relationship between yin and yang, or between the *unconscious* and the *conscious*. In other words, the *conscious* is inversely proportional to the *unconscious*. Whenever the former grows the latter decreases, and whenever the former decreases the latter increases. Moreover, they are in a reverse movement. Thus the relationship between the *conscious* and the *unconscious* in all other forms of archetype is mutually complementary and interdependent. This kind of relationship assures us again that anything that is real must be a "both-and" relationship rather than an "either-or". To separate one from the other is in fact to deny the reality of them altogether. Therefore, whenever we say that the *conscious* is, we cannot avoid mentioning its counterpart, that is, the *unconscious*. Whenever we mention the physical body, we also have to mention the existence of its counterpart, that is, the spiritual body. Since the *conscious* is analogous with the physical body and the *unconscious* with the spiritual body, the relationship between these bodies is in an inverse proportion. Whenever the physical body manifests itself, apparently the spiritual body retreats to be the background of the former. Whenever the spiritual body manifests itself clearly at death, the physical body becomes ineffective. Therefore, we can conclude that both the physical body and the spiritual body or the *conscious* and the *unconscious* can be maintained, because they presuppose the existence of archetypes.

What do we mean by the archetypes of these bodies? According to Carl Jung, the idea of archetypes can be traced back as early as Plato's notion of forms (*eidola*), "in accordance with which the mind organizes its contents." [8] This idea of forms occurs as early as Philo-Judaeus with reference to the *imago dei* in man. However, Jung actually borrowed the idea of Augustine, who speaks of "principle" ideas which are not formed but eternally existing in the divine understanding. These principle ideas or *typical* images can be understood as archetypes. [9] These principle ideas or archetypes are abundant in comparative religion and mythology. However, archetypes are not the contents of archaic images. They are merely structures or forms without any specific content. Thus Jung says,

The archetypes are, so to speak, organs of the pre-rational psyche. They are eternally inherited forms and ideas which have at first no specific content. Their specific content only appears in the course of the individual's life, when personal experience is taken up in precisely these forms. [10]

These archetypes which are devoid of any content can continue their existence in spite of one's death. Jung thinks that it is a primordial and universal idea that the dead can continue their earthly existence without knowing that they have the archetypes. The archetypes without any content are often known as ghosts or shadows, etc., in primitive cultures. However, this does not mean that they are merely passive and helpless.

For, just as the organs of the body are not mere lumps of indifferent, passive matter, but are dynamic, functional complexes which assert themselves with imperious urgency, so also the archetypes, as organs of the psyche, are dynamic, functional complexes which assert themselves with imperious urgency, so also the archetypes, as organs of the psyche, are dynamic, instinctual complexes which determine psychic life to an extraordinary degree. That is why I also call them *dominants* of the unconscious. [11]

The archetypes which Jung describes are more than passive and static forms of psyche, but are the dynamic and functional complexes which give certain directions to all experiences. They are the basic drives and inclinations which are fundamentally responsible for personality development and character.

Even though the idea of archetypes comes from the Platonic view of static ontology, what Jung attempts to say is quite different. They are not merely forms and structures of pre-existence. They have dynamic and functional implications to existence. In other words, the archetypes have two specific characters: the structural basis for human existence and certain directions of movement or change for human destiny. These two main characteristics of archetypes are the dominants of the *unconscious* and the *conscious*. In fact, the archetype as the structural foundation for the *conscious* means no less than the center of meaning and unity of human existence. Thus it is the archetype of forms which sustains and produces the goals and aspirations as well as the images of heroes, gods, demons, monsters, spirits, and other archaic symbols. In other words, it is the structural aspect of the archetype which produces the archaic and primordial images for the unity of meaning of human existence. I believe this is the primary contribution of Carl Jung and Mircea Eliade when they speak of the archetypes. However, the archetypes have much more than image-producing functions. They are, to me, primarily the inclinations or certain trends of action and actualization. They are the primordial inclinations of individuation. They are the germinal essences of personality and character formation. These seed-energies of individuation are also known as the manifestations of individual *karmas*. Everyone has his own *karma*, because it is the essence of his existence. Thus, archetypes are similar to Leibnitz's notion of monads or the *I Ching's* idea of hexagrams. The hexagrams as the archetype possess both the structural units and the directional movements of individuation. Thus Richard Wilhelm remarked,

In the phenomenal world, each thing has its specific nature: this is the principle of individuation. At the same time this specific nature fixes a boundary that separates each individual being from every other. [12]

We may study carefully what the principles of individuation or the archetypes are in the light of hexagrams in the *I Ching*.

The hexagrams in the *I Ching* are understood as the microcosms of the universe. They are not only the basic forms for phenomenal existence in all things but also the germinal situations of possible becoming. Everything in the world can be reduced to one of the hexagrams, because everything is of yin and yang. The hexagrams are then the basic units of the yin and yang relationship. Since both of them are units of individuation, they can be called the archetypes. The hexagrams are not only the archetypes of human existence but also those of all other existence. We may examine how the hexagrams can function as the archetypes of man before we examine the different kinds of archetypes in the *I Ching*.

The hexagrams in the *I Ching* are the germinal situations or the seed-energies which are not yet actualized. That is why the hexagrams are essentially the archetypes of all things. As to man, they represent the archetypes of personality. Let us take two cardinal hexagrams and analyze their characteristics as the archetypes of personality. The cardinal hexagrams among 64 in the *I Ching* are the first and second hexagrams, which are called the *Ch'ien* and *K'un* or the Creative and Responsive. [13] The former has the image of heaven and the latter the image of earth. The former is the archetype of masculine personality, and the latter that of feminine personality. All other archetypes or hexagrams are relative to these two archetypes. As you will notice from the symbols of these two hexagrams, they are opposite in character. The basic constituents of *Ch'ien* are all yang, while those of *K'un* are all yin. Yang characterizes the active and light principle, while yin the passive and dark principle. Thus *Ch'ien* archetype is basically a norm of an extrovert personality, while *K'un* is fundamentally a norm of an introvert personality. Thus within these two poles all other types of personality will appear. Even though there are 64 different forms of archetypes in the *I Ching*, the actual number of archetypes is not important. However, there is a metaphysical implication to the numerical significance of 64. [14] Just as more than a hundred different atomic structures are known in our time, the classification of personality does not have to be limited within 64 basic types. However, let us suppose, as the *I Ching* attempts to say, that there are 64 archetypes of personality available in the universe. If we look at some of these archetypes of personality, we can notice that the metaphysical principle controls their characteristics. For example, the third hexagram is *Chun* (屯), or "Difficulty at the Beginning", or the personality of slow acquaintance. The archetype of *Chun* consists of two yang lines and four yin lines as we see from the symbol of hexagram.

This carries the images of clouds and thunder, which are based on the structural formation of two trigrams. By simply looking at the structure of yin and yang, we notice how difficult the yang principle or the active and outward character on the first place faces the difficulty of adjusting with the powerful yin principles on the second, third, and fourth places. However, even though it is difficult at first, the yang line is again located on the central position, which is at the fifth place. Thus later on things go easily and smoothly. We see many people who have this kind of personality. They are difficult to get to know at first, but when we get to know them, they are often not only friendly but also well-adjusted people. Let us look at the fifteenth hexagram, *Ch'ien* (謙), which means modesty. This archetype represents the person of humble character. The image of this hexagram is a mountain within the earth. A mountain usually stands above the earth, but when it is under it, it is the symbol of lowliness. The judgment of this hexagram reads, "Modesty creates success. The superior man carries things through." [15] When the superior man is humble, he is not only a mature person but achieves great work. Thus, Jesus said,

Whosoever shall exalt himself shall be abased; and he that shall humble himself shall be exalted. (Matthew 23:12.)

It is said in the Old Testament, "God resists the proud, but gives grace to the humble." (James 4:6.)

Some of these examples help us to understand how the hexagrams, as the microcosms of the universe, can represent the archetypes of personality. They not only indicate the images they represent but also give us their basic characters and inclinations. As we have seen, the symbols of the hexagram convey the structural meaning of the germinal situations or the archetypes. On the other hand, the judgments or *t'uan*, which are brief texts which accompany hexagrams, usually indicate the directions of movement or the inclinations of a particular archetype. Therefore, the hexagrams as the archetypes of personality seem to have both the primordial structures of human existence and the basic inclinations of their evolvement toward their actualization. They represent the germinal energies which are not yet fully actualized. For the actualization of their potency, the judgment or *t'uan* gives a certain instruction or indication of either good or bad outcome of the future. Therefore, the hexagrams are idealistic forms of representation for the archetypes of personality.

From what we have observed so far, we can see that the archetypes of personality as expressed in the hexagrams are delimited by a definite number of yin and yang. In other words, all the hexagrams have 6 lines of either yin or yang. Thus all the archetypes of personality in the *I Ching* are identical in quantity. This means human beings are equal regardless of their differences in personality. However, a man can change from one archetype to another archetype but never creates a new archetype. The change of personality is none other than the transformation of one to another form of archetype. How can he transform from one to another archetype? In order to illustrate the change of archetypal personality, let us take up the hexagrams 13 and 30. The hexagram 13 is *T'ung Jen* (同人), which means friendship. The hexagram 30 is *Li* (離), which means conforming or clinging. *T'ung Jen* represents the archetype of friendly personality, while *Li* is the archetype of conforming personality. We see the similarity between these two personalities, even though they are quite different. If we look at the structures of their hexagrams, we can visualize their differences much more clearly. As we see, the hexagram *T'ung Jen* has only one yin line on the second place and the rest of them are yang lines. Thus it is closely related to the archetype of *Ch'ien* or

T'UNG JEN   LI

the Creative, which has all yang lines. When we look at the hexagram *Li* or the Conforming, it has one more yin line than the hexagram *T'ung Jen*. The fifth line of *T'ung Jen* changed to yin from yang. Thus *Li* hexagram means conformity, which is closely related to friendship. Since yang or creative force is lacking in *Li*, it expresses the passive form of friendship, that is, conformity. On the other hand, the active and creative form of conformity is friendship, because there is one more yang in it. Furthermore, the passive form of *Ch'ien*, or the true Creativity, is expressed in friendship or *T'ung Jen*. Thus personality can change from one archetype to another through the change of either yin or yang elements. As we see, the archetype of friendly personality, or *T'ung Jen*, changes to the archetype of conforming personality, or *Li* by changing a yang element to a yin element in the fifth place, which is the governing position of this hexagram.

There are two factors to be considered when the archetype is transformed. The first factor deals with the change of either yang to yin or yin to yang As we have seen, the change of yang to yin results in a change to a new personality. When yang changes to yin, a more passive form of personality results. When yin changes to yang, then it becomes a more active personality. Thus the character of personality is controlled by the change of line or lines between yin and yang. Another factor deals with the location of the changing line. Let me take up the hexagram 37, *Chia Jen* (家人), to illustrate the importance of the location of the changing line. As we see, *Li* and *Chia Jen* have the identical numbers of yin and yang lines, but they don't have the

CHIA JEN

identical structure. When the fifth line of *T'ung Jen*, or the archetype of friendly personality, changes to yin from yang, it changes to *Li*, or the archetype of conforming personality. However, when the fourth line of the same hexagram changes to yin from yang, it changes to *Chia Jen*, which means literally "the family man." *Chia Jen*, then, means the archetype of family-oriented personality, which is a more passive form of fellowship than friendship of *T'ung Jen*. We see clearly the importance of location or position of the changing line, which deals with the structural aspect of archetypes. On the other hand, the change of yang to yin or yin to yang deals with the characteristic aspect of archetypes. Therefore, the change of archetypes is due to the transformation not only of either yin to yang or yang to yin, but also of structural position. To attain a certain archetype of personality, both the structural and functional balances are necessary. Again, we are reminded of the importance of both the basic structure and the archaic impulse or character in our understanding of archetypes of personality.

Let us then summarize our discussion by relating the archetypes to both the *conscious* and the *unconscious* as well as to the physical body and the spiritual body. As we have seen, the hexagram as the archetype of personality means, first of all, the delimitation of its quantity. It cannot have more than 6 lines of either yin or yang. Thus the change of the *conscious* to the *unconscious* or the *unconscious* to the *conscious* is inversely proportioned. In other words the archetype can be compared with a sealed container where the change of the *conscious* is inversely proportioned to the change of the *unconscious*. Thus, when the *conscious* grows, the *unconscious* decreases. When the *unconscious* grows, the *conscious* decreases. Thus no new thing is added to the archetype. To illustrate it, for example, water in a sealed container can change to steam, and the steam to the water again. Sometimes there is more water than steam, and other times there is more steam than water. But no new steam or water is added to the container. Likewise, the change of the *conscious* to the *unconscious* and the *unconscious* to the *conscious* is possible within a certain structure of archetype. What does it mean? It means that both the *conscious* and the *unconscious* are the manifestations of the archetype of personality. The *conscious* is none other than the *conscious* manifestation of a certain archetype, and the *unconscious* of the same person is the *unconscious* manifestation of the same archetype. Therefore, we can say that the archetype which is *conscious* is also the same archetype which is *unconscious* at the same time. In other words, the archetype of personality is *both* the *conscious* *and* the *unconscious* at the same time. If we connect the *conscious* with life and the *unconscious* with death, the archetype of personality is present in *both* life *and* death simultaneously. If it is present in both life and death, it is the eternal reality, the eternal inherent form. Thus, it is said,

The eternal conscious self (archetype) is not born, never dies; it does not come from anywhere, nothing is born from it. Unborn, eternal, everlasting, the ancient one is not destroyed when the body is destroyed. [16]

The archetype of personality is much more than a mere form or structure. It is also dynamic, that is, it has the direction of movement and the impulse of unity. This dynamic aspect of direction and unity coincides with the passive aspect of form and structure to make the archetype of personality retain its principle of individuation in the midst of the ever-flowing and changing phenomena of the universe.

To conclude our study of the existence of the spiritual body after death from the Eastern point of view, it is rather significant to mention that the existence of the spiritual body is often claimed by the "out-of-the-body" experiences as witnessed by contemporary authors.

A number of modern authors have written accounts of out-of-the-body and mystical experiences, some of them autobiographical. Among them in the last century were Wordsworth, Emily Bronte, George Eliot, George Meredith, and Tennyson; and in this century, Arnold Bennett, D. H. Lawrence, Virginia Woolf, Warner Allen, Bernard Tserenson, John Buch, William Gerhartdi, Koestler, and Hemingway. After he had been badly wounded, Hemingway wrote . . . "I felt my soul or something coming out of my body, like you'd pull a silk handkerchief out of a pocket by one corner. I flew around and came back and went back again and I wasn't dead anymore." [17]

There seems to be more scientific evidence for this spiritual body than we normally understand.

In 1968, Doctors V. Inyushim, V. Grishehenke, N. Vorobev, N. Fedorova, and F. Gibadulim announced their discovery: All living things — plants, animals and humans — not only have a physical body made of atoms and molecules, *but also a counterpart body of energy*. They called it "the Biological Plasma Body." [18]

Moreover, the Kirlian discovery has opened up the possibility of new dimensions in the understanding of the spiritual body or the counterpart body. [19] Therefore, it is helpful to hear the advice of H. H. Price who says,

Do not be too sure that you will not continue to exist as a person after your physical organism has died.[20]

NOTES AND REFERENCES

[1] I Cor. 15:44.

[2] Munadaka Upanishad, III, 1,1.

[3] Fan Chen (范縝), (ca. 450-c515), *Shen Mieh Lun* (神滅論) in *Hun-Ming Chi* (弘明集) by Seng-yu (僧祐), Chap. 9, pp.30, 38.

[4] Aubrey R. Johnson, *The Vitality of the Individual in the Thought of Ancient Israel* (2nd Ed., Cardiff: University of Wales Press, 1964), p. 88.

[5] Rabindranath Tagore, *The Religion of Man* (Boston, Beacon Press), pp. 145-6.

[6] W. Y. Evans-Wentz, Ed., *The Tibetan Book of the Dead* (New York: Oxford University Press, 1960), p. 34.

[7] For the symbol of this hexagram, see Chap. III, p. 27.

[8] Carl Jung, "Psychological Commentary," in *The Tibetan Book of the Dead*, p. xliv.

[9] Carl Jung, *The Collected Works of C. G. Jung* (New York: Pantheon Books), IX, 1, 4; VII, 136.

[10] Carl Jung, "Psychological Commentary," in *The Tibetan Book of the Dead*, p. xliv.

[11] *Ibid.*, p. xlv.

[12] *The I Ching: The Richard Wilhelm Translation*, p. 378.

[13] For the symbols of hexagram *Ch'ien* and *K'un*, see Chap. III, pp. 25, 27.

[14] For a comprehensive treatise on the significance of 64 hexagrams, see J. Y. Lee, *Principle of Changes*, pp. 143ff.

[15] *The I Ching: The Richard Wilhelm Translation*.

[16] Katha Upanishad, I, ii, 18.

[17] Quoted by Susy Smith in *The Enigma of Out-of-the-Body Travel* (New York: Helix Press, 1965), p. 22; Hemingway made use of this experience in Chap. 9 of his *A Farewell to Arms*.

[18] Sheila Ostrander and Lynn Schroeder, *Psychic Discoveries Behind the Iron Curtain* (Englewood: Prentice-Hall, 1970), p. 213.

[19] *Ibid.*, pp. 215ff.

[20] H. H. Price, "The Problem of Life After Death," in *Religious Studies*, 3, no. 2 (April 1968), p. 459.

5 An Understanding of the After-Death State

The Study of the *Bardo* Phenomena

What would be the experience of the after-death state? Perhaps this is the perennial question which may not be fully answered. Even though this question persists in the minds of the living, speculation is often discouraged about the possible means of understanding this experience. One of the typical answers to the possibility of investigating the experience of the after-death state is:

No one can ever talk about the experience of after-death, because nobody has ever returned from death.

How could we know what kind of experience the dead go through unless we returned from death? For this question, those who are oriented toward the "both-and" way of thinking will say:

There is no *one* person, indeed, no *one* living being, that has not returned from death. In fact, we all have died many deaths, before we came into this incarnation. [1]

As long as we think in the "either-or" way of classification following the axiom of Aristotelian logic, we cannot even discuss the possibility of knowing the experience of the after-death state. As long as we base our understanding of reality on the means of discrimination of this from that, we cannot understand the reality as a whole. The knowledge of a part of the whole does not lead to the knowledge of the whole. Rather, the understanding of the whole may lead to the understanding of a part of that whole. The whole is not known by the sum of its parts. Thus, our reality is to study a part from the whole, rather than from a part to the whole.

As the study of death par excellence, the *Bardo Thödol* presupposes the complementary relationship between the experience of life and the experience of the after-death state. Death is the other side of life, and life is the other side of death. The former is the background of the latter. Thus what is experienced in life will be revealed after death. Life experience deals with the state of consciousness in living, while the death experience deals with the reverse phenomenon of life experience. In other words, the *Bardo*, or the after-death plane, is a reversal of life. The readings on the first day of the second stage of the *Bardo* period begin as follows:

O nobly-born, thou hast been in a swoon during the last three and one-half days. As soon as thou are recovered from this swoon, thou wilt have the thought, "What hath happened!" Act so that thou wilt recognize the *Bardo*. At that time, all the *Sangsāra* will be in revolution. [2]

The *Sangsāra* experience is the phenomenal experience of life, which is to be revealed after death in a reverse order. As Evans-Wentz comments,

Phenomena, or phenomenal experiences as experienced when in the human world, will be experienced in quite another way in the *Bardo* world, so that to one just dead they will seem to be in revolution or confusion; hence the warning to the deceased, who must accustom himself to the after-death state as a babe must accustom itself after birth to our world. [3]

We see the correlation between the life experience and death experience, even though it is in the order of revolution. Just as both birth and death are analogous, the experience of a newly-born baby and that of one newly dead are identical, even if their directions of movement are quite opposite. We see their relationship as analogous with that of yin and yang. Since the life experience represents yang and the death experience yin, they are complementary to each other. The movement of yang is the reverse order of yin. When yang increases, yin decreases. When yang decreases, yin grows at the same time. When yang goes upward, yin goes downward; when yang goes downward, yin goes upward. In this way the directions of their movement are reversed. Thus the dead will see his life experience in a reverse order, or the order of revolution. Our life experience in a thought form is preserved more or less in the form of a movie film, which is to be seen again by us in the *Bardo* world when we die. The death experience or the experience which the dead will have is nothing new, but the same experience of his life projected in the forms of visions, images, and pictures on the mental screen of the dead. Thus the dead sees the experience of his own life in the form of a picture. However, the dead cannot see the picture of his life in the same order as life but in a reversed and confused order. The dead no longer sees his life from birth to death but sees it from death to birth, since the film is projected in a reversed order. Moreover, it is projected in a reverse direction. As Saher said,

It is as difficult for the dead person to see through the *karmic* impression [the film of his life] which is presented, as it is for a living person to accompany the projected light backwards into the lamp. [4]

That is why the dead one has to readjust his perspective when he sees the movie of his own life in the *Bardo* World. Because death and life are mutually inclusive and interdependent, death is experienced in life and life in death. This continuum between death and life also provides the continuum between the dead and the living in their *Bardo* experience. In other words, the *Bardo* world which the dead one experiences can also be experienced by the living. The *Bardo Thödol* says that there are six different ways the *Bardo* world is to be experienced:

There are six states of *Bardo*, namely: the natural state of *Bardo* while in the womb; the *Bardo* of the dream-state; the *Bardo* of ecstatic equilibrium, while in deep meditation; the *Bardo* of the moment of death; the *Bardo* [during the experiencing] of Reality; the *Bardo* of the inverse process of *sangsaric* existence. These are the six. [5]

The last three *Bardo* experiences deal with the experience of the dying, death, and reincarnation. The *Bardo* of the moment of death is called the *Hchi-khahi* or *Chi-khai Bardo*. The characteristic of this *Bardo* is the dawning of the Clear Light of the Void, which is the radiant energy of *Dharma-Kāya*, the highest and unspeakable Bodhi-body, or formless. This is the period of the so-called "swoon", so that the dead is unconscious of the light. It corresponds in life to the period from birth to about three years of age. During the life of infancy the baby usually does not memorize his life at all. The *Bardo* of Reality comes right after the *Bardo* of the moment of death. This *Bardo* is the *Chö-nyid Bardo*, which is the moment of experiencing the reality of death. In this period the dead one can review his life experience in visions and images as though they are projected in the film on the screen. This *Bardo* corresponds in life to the most active period of life. The *Bardo* of the inverse process of *sangsāric* experience, or seeking rebirth, is known as the *Sidpa Bardo*, which follows immediately after the *Chönyid Bardo*. The process of reincarnation begins with this *Bardo*. Thus it corresponds roughly to the old age of life. It is the period of inclination toward the inverse order. This *Bardo* is followed by "the *Bardo* while in the womb", which is known as the *Kye-nay Bardo*. This *Bardo* deals with the intermediate state of man right before his birth. Thus it corresponds to *Chikhai Bardo*. The rest of two *Bardos* are capable of being experienced in life. They are the *Bardo* of the dream-state, which is known as *Mi-lam Bardo*, and the *Bardo* of the ecstatic equilibrium while in deep meditation, which is also called the *Tin-ge-zin Sam-tam Bardo*. The former is known to all the living at night, while the latter is known to a particular group of people who practice *yoga*. In our time, with the use of mescaline and LSD, the similar experience of the *Tin-ge-zin Sam-tan Bardo* can be created, even though its authenticity is questioned. [6] Perhaps we may be able to introduce one more *Bardo*, the *Bardo* of the drug-induced state, which may include the experience of psychosis. Even though there are six or seven different forms of *Bardo* experience, they are intrinsically identical. All of them are the experience of "the other side of life." Thus the *Bardo* experience is the other side of the *Sangsāric* experience. Since the experience of death commonly includes the *Chikhai Bardo* (of the moment of death), the *Chonyid Bardo* (of Reality) and the *Sidpa Bardo* (of seeking rebirth), we can experience it through our experience of the *Bardo* of the dream-state, as well as through deep meditation and the drug-induced state. There are not many Westerners who are used to practicing the form of deep meditation. However, there are increasing numbers of youth who have taken mescaline and LSD in recent times. Thus it is useful at least to be aware of the phenomena of the mental conditions of the drug-induced state, which are quite similar to what the *Bardo Thödol* attempts to describe as the experience of the after-death state.[7] Moreover, the *Bardo* experience in our dream-state is available to all the living. Thus by understanding our experience of the dream-state and the drug-induced state, we may understand the characteristics of the after-death experience in life.

As we have indicated, all the different kinds of *Bardo* experience are essentially the same, even though they are different in existence and in their intensity. "Dreams are spontaneous products of the unconscious."[8] Thus by analyzing our dream experience we may be able to understand the real experience of death. The experience of dreaming is like other *Bardo* experiences; it is the experience of the *unconscious*, which differentiates the *Bardo* from the *Sangsāric* experience. In other words, the *Bardo Thödol*, as the excellent book on a phenomenological study of death, presupposes the complementary relationship between the experience of the *unconscious* and the experience of the *conscious*. The dream-state is the other side of the awakening state. In the dream-state the *unconscious* is active and the *conscious* is inactive, and in the awakening state the *conscious* is active and the *unconscious* is inactive. We see the same relationship between the experience of life and the experience of death. They are inversely proportional. The dream-state belongs to the realm of darkness, that is, yin, while the awakening state belongs to the realm of light, that is, yang. Just as death is yin, the dream-state is yin. Just as life is yang, the awakening state of day is yang. Thus the experience of death corresponds to the experience of the dream-state, and the experience of life corresponds to that of the awakening state. That is why from early times the analogous relation between sleep and death has been made consistently. As Hamlet speaks of death,

For in that sleep of death what dreams may come when we have shuffled off this mortal coil.[9]

Death is often called the eternal sleep.

Paul, for example, speaks of death as "sleep". He and other New Testament writers hold the view that, after sleeping, "the dead will be raised imperishable" (I. Cor. 15:32 RSV) on the day of resurrection.[10]

Oscar Cullmann, one of the outstanding New Testament scholars, said

that the inner man, who has already been transformed by the Spirit (Rom. 6:3ff.), and consequently made alive, continues to live with Christ in this transformed state, in the condition of sleep.[11]

Then, the analogy between death and sleep is not only an Eastern but also a Western notion.

It is a commonly accepted idea that the child often associates sleep with death when he goes to bed. His intuitive feeling of associating death with sleep has something to do with the reality of both death and the dream-state. That is why, as Saher said,

as life is *like* a dream, dream-like phenomena occurring after death cannot be intrinsically different from similar phenomena during life before death. [12]

Just as the dream-state is created by the dreamer who dreams, the life after death is also produced by the dead who lived his life. That is why no one can tell what kind of experience the dead is going to go through. The contents of the after-death experience are different to different persons, just as the contents of dreams are different to dreamers. Thus, Evans-Wentz remarks:

Rationally considered, each person's after-death experiences, as the *Bardo Thödol* teaching implies, are entirely dependent upon his or her own mental content. In other words, as explained above, the after-death state is very much like a dream state, and its dreams are the children of the mentality of the dreamer. This psychology scientifically explains why devout Christians, for example, have had — if we are to accept the testimony of Christian saints and seers — visions in a trance or dream state or in the after-death state of God the Father seated on a throne in the New Jerusalem, and of the Son at His side, and of all Biblical scenery and attributes of Heaven, or of the Virgin and Saints and archangels, or of purgatory and hell. [13]

Lama Govinda agrees with him and says,

The illusory *Bardo* visions vary, in keeping with the religious or cultural tradition in which the percipient has grown up, but their underlying motive-power is the same in all human beings. [14]

The *Bardo Thödol*, thus, teaches the mosaic of the structure, not the contents, as the after-death experience, even though its illustrations are based on the Tantric Buddhism. Just as the structure of a dream can be explained through the use of imaginary seeing, feeling, and hearing, the *Bardo Thödol* is more interested in the structural aspect of the after-death experience. Here, we see the inclusive non-dogmatic assertions of this book, which proves to be an excellent study of the inclusive understanding of death.

What then makes the *Bardo* experience possible? For this question, the *Bardo Thödol* again presupposes the existence of the spiritual body as the counterpart of the physical body. Without presupposing the existence of the spiritual body there is no way for the dead to continue the *Bardo* world after death. The spiritual body as incorruptible is affirmed in the New Testament. Cullmann says,

An incorruptible body! . . . Paul says in Phillippians 3:21 that at the end Christ will transform our lowly body into the body of his own glory (*doxa*), just as in II Corinthians 3:18: "We are being transformed into his own likeness from glory to glory (*apo doxes eis doxan*)." [15]

The *Bardo Thödol* seems to confirm the idea of the radical transformation of the physical body to the spiritual body at the moment of death. The tremendous release of energy at this transition appears as radiant light in different colors. The radiant energies from the various psychic centers of the body are quite evident at the transition of the body from the physical to the spiritual. Because the spiritual body is the embodiment of the *unconscious*, it presupposes the archetypal structure and the archaic impulse of the *unconscious* self. It is a grave mistake to identify the spiritual body, the counterpart of the physical body, with the idea of *karma* in the *Bardo Thödol*. The spiritual body deals with the archetype of personality, while the individual *karma* deals only with the archaic impulse of that body. Thus the former includes the latter. *Karma* is the vehicle of reincarnation of the dead and the impulse of ego-consciousness. Carl Jung calls *karma* psychic heredity. He said,

According to the Eastern view, *karma* implies a sort of psychic theory of heredity based on the hypothesis of reincarnation, which in the last resort is an hypothesis of the supra-temporality of the soul. . . . Hence we may cautiously accept the idea of *karma* only if we understand it as *psychic heredity* in the very widest sense of the word. [16]

It is perhaps better to say that psychic heredity is possible because of *karma*, rather than to identify them together as Jung as done. Certainly, the continuity between the physical body and the spiritual body is possible because of *karma*, the archaic impulse of individuation and regression. The distinction between the spiritual body and *karma* ought to be made in the *Bardo Thödol*, because to be liberated from the chain of birth and death means to break off from *karma*, not from the spiritual body. The spiritual body must be retained even after liberation. The Christian idea of the resurrection of the spiritual body seems to make sense in the light of this differentiation in the *Bardo Thödol*.

One who reads the *Bardo Thödol* soon notices that the constant instruction of the guru for the dead or the dying is to discriminate between dull lights and clear lights. The dull lights represent the *karmic* illusions, while the clear lights represent the reflections of the cosmic unconsciousness. Both of them appear to be dead, side by side, as soon as the first *Bardo* or the *Chikhai Bardo* is over. This double parallel presentation of lights signifies the dead being in the world of duality. There is a *Nirvanic* line symbolized by the various bright colors of different divinities. There is also a *Sangsāric* line, which is symbolized by the various colors of dull lights coming from six different *lokas* or worlds. As the text says,

O nobly born, along with the radiances of Wisdom, the impure illusory lights of the Six *Lokas* will also come to shine. If it be asked, "What are they?" they are a dull white light from the *devas*, a dull green light from the *asuras*, a dull yellow light from human beings, a dull blue light from the brutes, a dull reddish light from the *pretas*, and a dull smoke-colored light from Hell. These six thus will come to shine, along with the six radiances of Wisdom; whereupon, be not afraid of nor be attracted towards any, but allow thyself to rest in the non-thought condition. [17]

The different colors and *lokas* of both the dull and the clear lights are correlated with the psychic centers of the body of the dead. Here, the micro-macrocosmic world view is supposed. The universe is an organic entity where everything is interdependent with one another. There is no essential difference between mind and matter.

Mind and matter are eternally the same. As the essence of matter is wisdom, the essence of matter is without form and is called the embodiment of wisdom. [18]

The universe is not an empty place but filled with the immeasurable *Pusas* and the immeasurable psychic energies available to man. Space is then none other than a mode of particularization being created by the power of change. As Evans-Wentz said, "Space therefore exists only in relation to our particularizing consciousness." [19] Each individual of this kind in the world is a microcosm of the universe, so that his psychic and nerve centers are correlated with the *Lokas* of the universe. We see the similarity of this kind of world view with the world of the *I Ching*, where the hexagrams represent the microcosmic world. Furthermore, the correlation of six *Lokas* with six lines of hexagrams is amazingly similar. The six *lokas* of the world in the *Bardo Thödol* deal with the totality of psychic layers of man and the completion of the universe. Likewise, in the *I Ching* the six lines imply the completion of the situation and the totality of the unit as a whole. Because of the six degrees of evolvement for the completion of the germinal archetype, it is called the hexagram, which means the image of six. We also see that the *Bardo Thödol*, like the *I Ching*, presupposes the complementary dualism. The duality of lights seems to co-exist without real conflict. The dull lights come from the empirical self, which is associated with *karma*, and the clear lights come from the true Self, which is associated with *Dhyāna*. Even though they are conflicting in existence, they are not conflicting in essence.

In the final analysis, however, all pairs of opposites being viewed as having a Single Source — in the Voidness of the *Dhārma-Kaya* — the apparent dualism becomes monism. [20]

This non-dualism in a noumenal sense is the basis of parascientific approach to the reality of life and death.

In the world of micro- and macrocosmic relations, the *Bardo Thödol* could easily relate the cosmic structure to the *Bardo* situations. We see the constant reappearance of numbers such as number 3, 5, and 49. These numbers are significant to the *Bardo* phenomena, because of their cosmic significances. We may take them separately and examine the cosmic significance to the *Bardo* phenomena.

As we have already indicated, the number 3 is important in the phenomena of the *Bardo* state, because three different *Bardos* are clearly indicated as the after-death state in the *Bardo Thödol*. Three *Bardos* are correlated to the three bodies of Buddha, which are often known as the Buddhist Trinity. They represent the bodies of cosmic Buddha, which could be said to be the collective unconscious, if we use Carl Jung's definition in a very liberal sense. They are the source of all the clear lights which the dead one sees in his *Bardo* journey. These three bodies of Buddha are the sources of enlightenment and guides for the Buddhist. For Christians there is the God of Trinity, which is practically similar with the Buddhist idea of *Tri-Kāya*. The Trinitarian God is the source of salvation to the Christians. Just as they have the God of Father, Son, and Holy Spirit, the Buddhist Trinity has three specific forms of manifestation. They are the *Dharma-Kāya*, the highest of all three bodies, the *Sambhoga-Kāya*, the body of perfect endowment, and the *Nirmāna-Kāya*, the body of incarnation. The *Dharma-Kāya* is more like the Brahman, who is beyond the description of human words. It is a formless body, the essence of the universe. The only way to express it is to use the famous formula employed by Yajnavalkya: *Neti, neti* — Not this, not this. [21] It is the realm of pure Mind and Consciousness.

The first *Bar'o* of death is followed by the coming of the radiant illumination of this body. The second *Bardo* is followed by the coming of the illumination of *Sambhoga-Kāya*, which is the body of perfect manifestation of the essential Wisdom. Because it is the manifestation of all perfect attributes of *Dharma-Kāya*, in the second *Bardo* the dead one visualizes the coming of various images of deities. The clear lights are no longer in the void but in the forms of deities. The final stage of *Bardo* is followed by the illumination of *Nirmāna-Kāya*, which means the body of reincarnation. Thus the process of reincarnation of the dead takes place in this *Bardo*. As we see, these three *Kāya* have been closely correlated to the three different planes of *Bardo* experience of the dead. The *Tri-Kāya* is the three-fold principle of the cause of all causes, which effects all things in the universe. It is the all-pervading essence of Spirit and Mind. We see the same implication made in China. The Trinity is expressed in the trigrams, which are bases for all 64 hexagrams, which represent every possible phenomenon of the universe. Thus the trigram or the trinity becomes the essence of all that is.

The number five has cosmological implications in the *Bardo Thödol*. Just as the doctrine of the three Bodies is correlated to the three stages of the *Bardo* state, the idea of five Dhyānī Buddhas is associated with the first five days of each *Bardo*. These five Wisdoms are the personified forms of universal divine attributes. The first day of the *Bardo* corresponds to the *Dharma-Dhātu*, blue in colour, shining, transparent, dazzling, from the heart of the Bhagavan Vairochana. [22] The *Dharma-Dhātu* is symbolized as the Aggregate of Matter, which is the beginning of all the creatures of this world. The second day of *Bardo* is correlated with the Mirror-like Wisdom, which is personified in Vajra-Sattva. This wisdom is associated with the element of water. As the text says,

The aggregate of thy principle of consciousness, being in its pure form — which is the Mirror-like Wisdom — will shine as a bright, radiant white light, from the heart of Vajra-Sattva, the Father-Mother, with such dazzling brilliancy and transparency that thou wilt scarcely be able to look at it, and will strike against thee. [23]

The third day of *Bardo* is correlated to the Wisdom of Equality, which is personified in Ratna-Sambhava, whose aggregate is touch. It represents the Earth-element, which produces the solid form of physical constituents. Thus, it is said,

On the Third Day the primal form of the element earth will shine forth as a yellow light. At that time, from the Southern Realm Endowed with Glory, the Bhagāvan Ratna-Sambhava, yellow in color, bearing a jewel in his hand, seated upon a horse-throne and embraced by the Divine Mother Sangyay-Chanma, will shine upon thee. [24]

The fourth day of *Bardo* is correlated with the All-Discriminating Wisdom, which is personified in the Dhyānī Buddha Amitābha. It is the aggregate of feeling, which is symbolized in a fire. The text reads,

The primal form of the aggregate of feelings as the red light of the All-Discriminating Wisdom, glitteringly red, glorified with orbs and satellite orbs, bright, transparent, glorious and dazzling, proceeding from the heart of the Divine Father-Mother Amitābha, will strike against thy heart so radiantly that thou wilt scarcely be able to look upon it. Fear it not. [25]

Finally, the fifth day of *Bardo* is correlated with the All-Performing Wisdom, which is personified in Amogha-Siddhi, who represents the aggregate of volition. It corresponds to the primal form of the element *air*. On the fifth day we read:

The primal form of the aggregate of volition, shining as the green light of the All-Performing Wisdom, dazzlingly green, transparent and radiant, glorious and terrifying, beautified with orbs surrounded by satellite orbs of radiance, issuing from the heart of the Divine Father-Mother Amogha Siddhi, green in color, will strike against thy heart so wondrously bright that thou wilt scarcely be able to look at it. Fear it not. [26]

These five Dhyānī Buddhas, who represent the five days of *Bardo* visions, are the personifications of five elements. These five elements of matter, water, earth, fire, and air have been thought to be the basic constituents of the universe. Thus they represent the whole universe. Moreover, each element is correlated to a different aspect of man. In this way the world is correlated to man and to the *Bardo* experience.

Let us finally discuss the significance of number 49 in the cosmology of the *Bardo Thödol*. The significance of 49 days of *Bardo* journey lies in cosmology. The 49 days of *Bardo* trip should not be taken literally. The symbolic number 49 comes from the cosmological significance of number 7.

The number seven is not only a sacred number in Judeo-Christian cosmology but also in Hindu-Buddhist cosmology. The number 49 is then the maximum expansion of the number seven, that is, seven times seven. Esoterically,

> there are seven worls or seven degrees of Māyā within the *Sangsāra*, constituted as seven globes of a planetary chain. On each globe there are seven rounds of evolution, making the forty-nine (seven times seven) stations of active existence. [27]

These forty-nine stations of active existence correspond to the forty-nine days of journey in the *Bardo*. Perhaps the best illustration of this kind of cosmogony is found in the central mountain of Hindu and Buddhist cosmography, the Mount Meru, which is regarded as the center of the Universe. It consists of the seven concentric circles of oceans separated by the intervening seven circles of golden mountains which support the entire universe. Here, the circles of seven oceans and seven mountains make the 49 stations of existence possible. We see the similar view of cosmography in the *I Ching*. There are sixty-four hexagrams or sixty-four germinal stations of existence in the universe. The number 64 comes from the 8 trigrams, which are expanded as far as possible to produce 64 (8 times 8). Whether it is 64 or 49, it represents the whole number, corresponding to the fullest evolution of cosmic phenomena. In the *Bardo* period the Sangsāric experience is fully and completely revealed in visions and images in an inverse order. Thus the forty-nine days of the *Bardo* period must be understood as the completion of involutionary attainments after death.

The significance of these numbers, as we have seen, is not in the numbers themselves. Their prime importance is the meaningful correlation of the *Bardo* structure with the structure of the universe. The correlation of cosmic structure to human existence as well as to Wisdom teachings is not a mere accident. In the world view of micro- and macrocosmic relationships, nothing is unrelated. Everything is correlated with the total structure of the universe. Everything is interdependent. Nothing can act independently of the total structure of the universe, which is a form of organism. Without presupposing this kind of world view it is not possible to describe the consequence of the after-death experience. Because of this correlation of every phenomenon of the world in terms of organic structure, the *Bardo Thödol* is more than guesswork. As Saher said,

> *The Tibetan Book of the Dead* is the first record we have of a *purely philosophical* attempt at a coldly scientific, reasoned analysis of the after-death state uncontaminated by guess work. [28]

NOTES AND REFERENCES

[1] Lama Anagarika Govinda, "Introductory Foreword," in *The Tibetan Book of the Dead*, Ed. by W. Y. Evans-Wentz (Oxford: Oxford University Press, 1960, p. liii.

[2] *The Tibetan Book of the Dead*, p. 105.

[3] *Ibid.*, note 1.

[4] P. J. Saher, *Eastern Wisdom and Western Thought* (New York: Barnes and Noble, 1970), p. 250.

[5] *The Tibetan Book of the Dead*, p. 102.

[6] See P. J. Saher, *op. cit.*, pp. 163ff.

[7] For detail see Timothy Leary, Ralph Metzner, and Richard Alpert, *The Psychedelic Experience: A Manual Based on the Tibetan Book of the Dead* (New Hyde Park, New York: University Books, 1964).

[8] Antonio Moreno, *Jung, Gods and Modern Man* (Notre Dame, Ind.: University of Notre Dame Press, 1970), p. 5.

[9] William Shakespeare, *Hamlet, Shakespeare's Principal Plays* (New York: The Century Co., 1927), p. 510.

[10] Milton McG. Gatch, "Some Theological Reflections on Death from the Early Church Through the Reformation," in *Perspectives on Death*, Ed. by Liston O. Mills (Nashville and New York: Abingdon Press, 1969), p. 100.

[11] Oscar Cullmann, "Immortality of the Soul or Resurrection of the Dead?" in *Immortality and Resurrection*, Ed. by Krister Stendahl (New York: Macmillan Paperbacks, 1967), p. 44.

[12] P. J. Saher, *op. cit.*, p. 247.

[13] *The Tibetan Book of the Dead*, p. 34.

[14] Lama Anagarika Govinda, *op. cit.*, p. lxii.

[15] Oscar Cullmann, *Immortality of the Soul or Resurrection of the Dead?* (London: The Epworth Press, 1958), p. 46.

[16] Carl Jung, *Psychological Commentary*, p. xliii.

[17] *The Tibetan Book of the Dead*, p. 124.

[18] *Ibid.*, p. 228.

[19] *Ibid.*, note 1.

[20] *Ibid.*, p. 121, note 4.

[21] Swami Nikhilananda, *The Upanishads*, Abridged Ed. (London: George Allen and Unwin, 1963), p. 33.

[22] *The Tibetan Book of the Dead*, p. 106.

[23] *Ibid.*, p. 109.

[24] *Ibid.*, pp. 110-111.

[25] *Ibid.*, p. 114.

[26] *Ibid.*, p. 116.

[27] *Ibid.*, p. 6.

[28] P. J. Saher, *op. cit.*, p. 248.

6 | The Experience of the Dying Moment

The Phenomena of the *Chikhai Bardo*

According to the *Bardo Thödol*, the moment of dying is called the *Chikhai Bardo*, or the intermediate state of the dying moment, which is regarded as being of the most crucial importance to the dying person. This crucial period is due to the radical transition from the physical body to the spiritual body or the ethereal body, from the *conscious* to the *unconscious*, or from the empirical self to the true Self at death. Since the principle of change presupposes a continuum in all opposites including the opposites of life and death, our approach to the phenomena of the *Chikhai Bardo* is to see death as the transition from one opposite to the other This transition is so radical that it is the most dangerous moment for the living to go through. Because of this danger the *Bardo Thödol* is written to instruct and initiate the dying person.

The *Chikhai Bardo* comes roughly after the final stage which Kübler-Ross calls the fifth stage of death. [1] After a persistent denial of death, accompanied by anger and depression, the dying person finally comes to accept death as inevitable. When the dying person approaches this stage, in most cases he is aware of the coming of his death. As Cicely Saunders says,

I know that some fifty per cent of my patients not only knew that they were dying but talked about it with me. Of the remaining fifty per cent, there were some who were senile, some who had cerebral tumors, and some who were just not able to have insight. There were others who, I think, recognized but did not choose to talk about it — at least not with me. [2]

It is, then, the intuition of the dying person to apprehend the inevitable outcome of his death. From the time of acceptance, the dying person may stay alive as long as seven days, even though usually about three or four days. [3] The *Chikhai Bardo* then begins as soon as the final stage of death is over.

The conditions of the dying person in the *Chikhai Bardo* are described by the common people as

55

the state wherein the consciousness-principle has fainted away. The duration of this state is uncertain. [It dependeth] upon the constitution, good or bad, and [the state of] the nerves and vital-force. In those who have had even a little practical experience of the firm, tranquil state of *dhyāna*, and in those who have sound nerves, this state continueth for a long time. [4]

As it is said, the duration of this *Bardo* is uncertain. It is primarily dependent on the mental and physical conditions of the dying person. However, the conditions of the dying described by the *Bardo Thödol* are very much similar to both the phenomenological death and thanatomimetic state. The phenomenological death is usually attributed to the dying phenomena where the conscious gives absolutely no indication of his continued existence, even though the body of organism is not dead. [5] On the other hand, thanatomimesis, which literally means the imitation of death, is attributed to something quite different. The thanatomimetic death means that the body of the organism appears to be dead but the mind or the conscious is actually alive. Because people are often unaware of the phenomenological and thanatomimetic states of death,

There have been many reports in medical, paramedical, and popular literature to the effect that people have been "taken for dead" and processed for burial when in fact they were still alive. [6]

This very last moment of death, or the *Chikhai Bardo*, seems to come when a yellowish liquid appears from the apertures of the dying body. It is said in the *Bardo Thödol* that the reading of instruction to the dying

is to be persisted in untill a yellowish liquid beginneth to appear from the various apertures of the bodily organs [of the deceased]. [7]

This is the very moment of death when the dying person is in the state of "swoon" and experiences the Clear Light of the Void. This moment may last only a minute or even long enough to be conscious of his death. It also depends on the mental and nerve conditions of the dying person. As it is said,

In those who have led an evil life, and in those of unsound nerves, the above state endureth only so long as would take a snap of a finger. Again, in some, it endureth as long as the time taken for the eating of a meal. [8]

Those who have practiced *yoga* could maintain in this kind of condition for a long time. Dr. Kastenbaum seems to recognize the effect of *yoga* to maintain the "self-induction of a thanatomimetic state as an exercise in 'mind-over-body' mastery." [9] The longer the dying person can maintain the condition of illumination by the Clear Light of the Void, the greater chance he has for enlightenment. That is why the proper attitude of the dying person at this crucial moment is most important.

It is commonly understood that a man at the last moment of death has fully uncovered himself from the masks he has worn in society. He does not have any mask with which to cover up. He cannot possess anything at the moment of death. He cannot take his wealth, his honor, his fame, or his knowledge. He who is dying is he who *is*, not he who has been. He takes nothing but his own self. The reality of his own nature is revealed at his death. He becomes natural to his own disposition. That is why the dying person looks natural and peaceful in most cases. I think Dr. Kübler-Ross describes it more eloquently than I can. She says:

Those who have the strength and the love to sit with a dying patient in the *silence that goes beyond words* will know that this moment is neither frightening nor painful, but a peaceful cessation of the functioning of the body. Watching a peaceful death of a human being reminds us of a falling star; one of a million lights in a vast sky that flares up for a brief moment only to disappear into the endless night forever. To be a therapist to a dying patient makes us aware of the uniqueness of each individual in this vast sea of humanity. [10]

Some of these words express vividly the beauty and peace of a dying moment. The process of death is the reversal of the process of birth. It is he who is born or is dying who must pass the stage by himself. He is naked, but rich with meaning. The sum of his life reveals at this moment the self. As Saunders has observed:

I recall so many who have been truly ready for meeting this "moment" . . . The reason why we are here is a summing up of everything that has happened before. At this stage, and I have seen it again and again, somehow there is a moment that is fully personal and everything is summed up. [11]

Because everything is summed up at the very moment of death,

Buddhists and Hindus alike believe that the last thought at the moment of death determines the character of the next incarnation. [12]

Thus the *Bardo Thödol* stresses the proper orientation of the last thought for the dying person. Whatever mental condition the dying person might have at the very moment of death, it is very likely retained in him even after death. That is why the guru speaks into the ears of the dying person so as to impress the sacred instruction upon his mind at the moment of death. It is important that the dying person is fully awake with a proper attitude of kind. As Krishna said to Arjuna,

One attaineth whatever state of being one thinketh about at the last when relinquishing the body. [13]

However, the mental attitude of the dying person does not arise instantly; it is the summation of his entire life.

The guru who repeats the instruction in the *Bardo Thödol* cannot produce a new mental disposition in the dying person. He can assist the dying person only if the latter can respond to the instruction with the sum of his selfhood. Thus man lives life for this moment of death. What he has been in life is disposed in this brief moment of death. We can compare the dying process with the process of diving into a deep abyss of water. Life can be compared with the diving board for the diver. The diving board exists solely for the preparation to dive. Just as the diver runs up to the end of the diving board for a jump, the dying person stands at the edge of life. When he comes to the end of the board, he must project himself as high as he can over the water. He has to accumulate the power of speed to make an effective dive. Likewise, the dying person prepares for his death in life. Unless he has accumulated a proper mentality in life, he cannot face the last moment of death peacefully and effectively. Those who are afraid of water cannot dive effectively. Likewise, those who are afraid of death cannot face the last moment of death positively. Those who are unwilling to die must learn the meaning of life. The art of living is also the art of dying. But, as Evans-Wentz said,

in the occident, where the Art of Dying is little known and rarely practiced, there is, contrastingly, the common unwillingness to die, which, as the *Bardo* ritual suggests, produces unfavorable results. As here in America, every effort is apt to be made by a materialistically inclined medical science to postpone, and thereby to interfere with, the death-process.[14]

The Art of Life without the Art of Dying is incomplete. It is the one-sidedness of Western civilization which has stressed the Art of Living alone. The Eastern perspective, that is, a "both-and" way, to human existence stresses *both* the Art of Living *and* the Art of Dying at the same time. It is the denial of *either* the Art of Living *or* the Art of Dying. Thus this "both-and" approach to man can help him prepare for the very moment of death.

Why is this last moment of death so crucial to the dying person? As we said, the life of the dying person is summed up in this crucial moment of death. When Pope John was dying, he said, "My bags are packed and I can go with a tranquil heart at any moment." [15] To use the analogy of the diver, he is ready to jump into the water. He comes to the end of the diving board and is ready to project himself over the water. His attitude, direction, and power which he has accumulated in life will eventually determine the effectiveness of his diving. What the dying person does at this moment of death will decide the destiny of his future existence. This is the most favorable moment for him to find life eternal or liberation from the chain of birth and death. At this moment the dying person can find the eternal "Thou", who is none other than the very essence of his own self, his inner Self. This is then his eternal homecoming. He can return in this very moment of death to his original home, the archetype of all his manifestations, which is his true Self. It is the liberation of himself from the *sangsāric* limitations and passions to the infinite Void of *Nirvāna* or the Kingdom of God. That is why it is also the moment of discovering his true Self, which has been deeply hidden in the abyss of his unconsciousness. If we describe it in religious terms, the dying person will find salvation in that last moment of death. How can he find liberation or salvation at that moment of death?

The *Bardo Thödol* teaches that the last moment of death or the *Chikhai Bardo* can reach the deepest abyss of unconsciousness. In other words, the true Self can be revealed directly to the dying person at the very moment of Death. When this *Bardo* is over, the Self is not revealed to the dead directly but only indirectly through images and visions. That is why the visions of peaceful deities and wrathful gods appear in the second and third stages of the after-death state. In the *Chikhai Bardo* the dying person does not see any visions, because the *karmic* illusions do not yet appear to him. He is in what is popularly called a "swoon", in which his empirical consciousness is totally nullified. In this "swoon" period the dying person does not see anything but the Clear Light of the Void, which illuminates th true Self or the Cosmic Unconsciousness. The text describes the Clear Light of the Void as follows:

Thy guru hath set thee face to face before with the Clear Light; and now thou art about to experience it in its Reality in the *Bardo* state, wherein all things are like the void and cloudless sky, and the naked, spotless intellect is like unto a transparent vacuum without circumference or centre. [16]

The light is the void, because it is formless. It is the colorless light, which is

beyond the light of sun, moon, and fire; to use the words of the Indian *Gita*. It is clear and colorless, but *māyik* [or form] bodies are colored in various ways. For color implies and denotes form. The formless is colorless. [17]

The Clear Light of the Void is then the most pure form of radiance illuminating from the highest form of reality, which is known as the *Dharma-Kāya*. By realizing the coming of this light, the dead is to be liberated from the *karmic* power, which creates in him the illusory desire to cling to the *sangsāric* experience. It demands courage, perhaps, on the part of the dying person to be united with the Clear Light of the Void. Just like the diver who must jump from the diving board without fear, the dying person must throw himself to that light if he is to be liberated. As Evans-Wentz said:

Faith is the first step on the Secret Pathway. Then comes illumination; and, with it, Certainty; and when the Goal is won, Emancipation. [18]

The dying person has to have enough faith to accept the Clear Light of the Void without fear. Since the awareness of the Clear Light of the Void is so important, the *Bardo Thödol* instructs the dying person to be fully awake at the moment of death. The guru attempts to keep the dying person conscious in spite of the failure of his nerve-center.

If the person dying be disposed to sleep, or if the sleeping state advances, that should be arrested, and the arteries pressed gently but firmly. [19]

By pressing the arteries the guru can keep the dying person awake. Unless he is awake, he cannot respond to the Clear Light of the Void. The light seems to come to the dying person when his expiration has ceased and the heart stops to beat. As the text says,

When the expiration hath ceased, the vital-force will have sunk into the nerve-center of Wisdom and the Knower will be experiencing the Clear Light of the Natural conditions. [20]

At this moment the body of the dying person should not be touched by others. In this critical moment the dying person alone is the captain of his own soul. No one should disturb or distract him by touching his body. It is not even allowed to have any unusual sound or object to distract the mental condition of the dying person.

During this time no relative or fond mate should be allowed to weep or to wail, as such is not good [for the deceased] ; so restrain them. [21]

It is better not to bother him. He who is dying must jump into the unknown world of his inner space. It is a sacred hour of death and the most delicate moment of self-liberation. In spite of this delicate moment of death, our technical civilization has failed to provide an adequate situation for the dying person.

Very often the dying is not permitted to die in his or her own home, or in a normal, unperturbed mental condition when the hospital has been reached. To die in a hospital, probably while under the mind-benumbing influence of some opiate, or else under the stimulation of some drug injected into the body to enable the dying to cling to life as long as possible, cannot but be productive of a very undesirable death, as undesirable as that of a shell-shocked soldier on a battle-field. [22]

In this kind of situation the dying person may not find the moment of calm and clear mental condition to concentrate on the appearance of the Clear Light of the Void. The failure of our Western civilization to provide the sacred moment of death can be attributed primarily to our valuing life only. We must not separate life from death so as to make them a dichotomy. Life and death are essentially inseparable. Without death there is no life, and without life neither is there death. They are mutually interdependent and complementary.

We may ask a question regarding the appearance of the Clear Light of the Void. Why does the light appear to the dying person? As we have already indicated, death does not mean the extinction of life. Rather, it means the transition of a physical body to its counterpart, which is the *Bardo* body or the spiritual body. By this radical transition from one pole to the other, both the radical disintegration of the physical body and the radical integration of the spiritual body takes place at the same time. In this very moment of transition, a tremendous intensity of energy is created. The intensity of energy radiation is greatest at the very moment of death.

The succeeding state is less intense. In the first, or primary stage, is experienced the Primary Clear Light, in the second stage, the Secondary Clear Light. A ball set bounding reaches its greatest height at the first bound; the second bound is lower, and each succeeding bound is still lower until the ball comes to rest.[23]

Since the most intense form of electromagnetic radiation comes to the dying person at the very moment of death or in the *Chikahi Bardo*, the light is pure and devoid of color and form. [24] It is not visible because of its intense radiation. According to the *Bardo Thödol*, the ethereal body or the spiritual body cannot see the light of the sun and moon and the stars, but is possible to see the astral light.

Only the natural light of nature (referred to by medieval alchemists and mystics as the "astral light") is to be seen in the after-death state; and this "astral light" is said to be universally diffused throughout the ether, like an earth twilight, yet quite bright enough for the eyes of the ethereally constituted beings in the *Bardo*. [25]

Thus the energy formed by the radical transition of the physical body to the ethereal body appears as the intensive form of astral light. Since the intensity of energy gradually decreases as the after-death state is prolonged, the intensity of astral radiation decreases. The decrease of its intensity means an increase of visibility and photosynthesis. Thus the dead experiences the decreasing intensity of light and growing numbers of different colors of illumination.

Why does the intensity of radiation energy decrease as the after-death state prolongs? This is a metaphysical question in which the *Bardo Thödol* is less interested. Since this book is written as a practical manual for the dying, we must seek the answer to this question from the *I Ching*, the standard work on this kind of metaphysics. In order to illustrate the decreasing intensity of radiation energy as the after-death state prolongs, let us examine the hexagrams which deal with the process of dying and death. The hexagram *Po*, "disintegration" or "splitting apart", has only one yang line (or the unbroken line) on the top and the rest of them are yin lines (or broken lines). [26] Thus the hexagram *Po* is the symbol of the approach of the dying moment. It is the disintegration of the yang principle. At the *Po* the consciousness-principle is at the verge of complete disintegration and the unconsciousness-principle is at the verge of complete integration. Thus, in this hexagram the process of both radical integration and radical disintegration has been initiated. Therefore, the *Chikhai Bardo*, or the very last moment of death, begins at the *Po*. The hexagram *K'un*, which signifies the primordial principle of responsivity, represents the state of complete disintegration of the consciousness-principle and the complete integration of the unconsciousness-principle. [27] Since there is no consciousness-principle in the hexagram *K'un*, it signifies the state in which the dead person is completely unconscious of his death. It is the state of "swoon", the deepest abyss of unconsciousness, which can be called the Collective Unconsciousness. The *K'un* represents the infinite possibility of response, since it is the source of all responsive attributes. The hexagram *Fu* signifies the appearance of one yang principle or the consciousness-principle in the ethereal body.[28]According to Evans-Wentz, the consciousness-principle is retained even in the ethereal body. [29] Here, we see the birth of the consciousness-principle in the ethereal body. The *Fu*, which literally means "returning" or "recovery", signifies the recovery of the dead from the "swoon", the total unconscious state. In the symbol of the hexagram *Fu*, its first line (or the bottom line) is the yang principle and the rest of them are yin principles. At the *Fu*, the dead is conscious of his death and experiences the reality of death. Thus with this hexagram the dead is ushered into the *Chönyid Bardo* or the intermediate state of experiencing the reality of death. When the consciousness-principle (or yang principle) increases, the *karmic* illusion also intensifies. Thus, when the dead comes to the hexagram *Lin*, he begins to approach to the process of reincarnation. [30] Thus the *Lin* means "approaching". At the *Lin* the dead begins to experience the third *Bardo* or the *Sidpa Bardo*, which means the stage of approaching reincarnation.

As a result we can observe that the increase of *karmic* illusions, which manifest themselves as the colorful visions and images of the dead, is proportional to the increase of yang or consciousness-principle in the ethereal body. For example, in the hexagram *K'un* there is no yang line or the consciousness-principle at all. Thus no visions and *karmic* illusions come to the *Bardo* body. However, in the hexagram *Fu* there is one yang or consciousness-principle. The *karmic* illusions in the form of various images and visions appear to the dead. When we come to the hexagram *Lin*, we see the increase of the consciousness-principle. This time there are two yang principles in the hexagram. Thus *karmic* powers have increased in the third *Bardo*. From these instances we can observe that the increase of the consciousness-principle in the *Bardo* body means the increase of the wavelength of radiation. Since the wavelength of radiation and the intensity of energy are inversely related, [31] the intensity of radiation energy, which is created by the radical transition at death, diminishes, as the *Bardo* body or the spiritual body gains more consciousness, and less radiation energy is available to the dead.

Why does the intensity of energy diminish as the consciousness-principle in the *Bardo* body increases? In order to answer it, let us consider the counterparts of these hexagrams we have examined. According to the principle of change in the *I Ching*, everything has its counterpart. [32] Nothing exists without its counterpart. Thus every hexagram has its own counterpart which is not manifested. Just as yin presupposes yang and yang presupposes yin, everything has its counterpart, for everything is none other than the constituent of yin and yang. Thus, we ought to include in our consideration the counterparts of those hexagrams we have discussed. In other words, each hexagram ought to be considered in relation to its counterpart. Thus let us see what are the counterparts of those hexagrams in relation to the *Bardo* periods. The hexagram *Kuai*, which means "break-through", is the counterpart of the hexagram *Po*. [33] The hexagram *Ch'ien*, which signifies the primordial principle of creativity, is the counterpart of the *K'un*, the primordial principle of responsivity. [34] The hexagram *Kou*, which means "coming to meet", is a counterpart of the *Fu* or "returning". [35] The hexagram *Tun*, which literally means "withdraw", is the counterpart of the *Lin* or "approaching". [36]

If we consider them together with their counterparts, we may be able to understand why energy is more available at the very moment of death than at any other stages of death. Let us first look at the hexagrams *Po* and *Kuai* together. As we have indicated, the hexagram *Po* is a symbol of the body of the dying person. The physical body is almost on the verge of complete disintegration. There is only one yang, or the vital force which keeps him alive. However, this vital force is at the verge of cessation. Thus the hexagram *Po* represents the weakest moment of a dying person. Since it presupposes its counterpart, the hexagram *Kuai* becomes its background. In other words, the hexagram *Kuai* is the background of the hexagram *Po*, and the latter is the foreground of the former. The background represents the potentiality of the foreground, and the foreground represents the actuality of the background. Therefore, when we look at the hexagram *Kuai*, it is full of energy. It has five yang or consciousness-principles. Thus the hexagram *Po* has the potentiality of responding to the vital energy of *Kuai*. The response to the active energy-power of *Kuai* by the *Po*, or the body of the dying person, means receiving five times more radiation energy than that of the body of the dying person. When we look at the hexagram *K'un*, which represents the moment of complete unconsciousness, it does not have any yang element or life-force at all. Thus, it represents the pure receptivity, for it has nothing but yin or receptive lines. Because of its pure receptivity, it presupposes the hexagram *Ch'ien*, the pure creativity, as its counterpart. Here, the infinite receptivity of *K'un* has the potentiality of receiving the infinite power of creative energy. That is precisely why, at the moment of death, the dead receives the Clear Light of the Void, the most intensive form of radiation coming from the most intensive energy of *Ch'ien*.

In the *I Ching*, both *K'un* and *Ch'ien* represent the primordial forms of receptivity and creativity. The rest of the hexagrams are none other than the products of these two primordial forms. Thus, in the *Chikhai Bardo* the dead receives the most intensive form of radiation. Here, the hexagram *Ch'ien* or the symbol of the primordial power of creativity represents the *Dharma-Kāya*, from which the Clear Light of the Void radiates. If the dying person at this last moment is totally receptive (as represented by the hexagram *K'un*) to the Clear Light of the Void, he is going to be in union with the *Dharma-Kaya*, the primordial body of Buddha, which is symbolized in the hexagram *Ch'ien*. However, the Clear Light of the Void does not come from outside of himself, because the *Ch'ien* is the background or the potentiality of the *K'un*. Thus, we can say that the *Ch'ien* or the *Dharma-Kāya* is the background of the *K'un* or the dead, and the latter is the foreground of the former. If we call the *Ch'ien* the Self, we can call the *K'un* the self. The Self is the background and the potentiality of the self, and the self is the foreground and actuality of the Self. Here, we see that both the receiver and the sender of the Clear Light of the Void are one. Thus the *Bardo Thödol* says:

Thine own intellect, which is now voidness, yet not to be regarded as of the voidness of nothingness, but as being the intellect itself, unobstructed, shining, thrilling, and blissful, is the very consciousness, the All-good Buddha. Thine own consciousness, not formed into anything, in reality void, and the intellect, shining and blissful — these two — are inseparable. The union of them is the *Dharma-Kāya* state of Perfect Enlightenment. [37]

When we see the hexagrams *Fu* and *Kou* together, the latter has the five yang or five active energy-principles which are receptive to the former. Since the former, that is, the *Fu*, in the *Chönyid Bardo* is receptive to the *Kou* which has lesser yang principles than the *Ch'ien*, the *Fu* receives lesser energy radiation than the *K'un* in the *Chikhai Bardo*. Therefore, the dead in the second *Bardo* begins to see the colorful visions and images, which are the manifestations of the weaker radiation energy than those of the Clear Light of the Void. Furthermore, the hexagram *Lin* in the third *Bardo* receives only four yang energy-principles of the *Tun*, which is weaker radiation energy than those of the *Kou* in the second *Bardo*. Thus, the available energy radiation in the *Bardo* becomes less and less when the *Bardo* state prolongs. On the other hand, as the *Bardo* period prolongs, the conscious energy in the *Bardo* body or the spiritual body increases. We may then conclude that the power of conscious energy in the spiritual body is inversely proportional to the power of radiation energy which comes to the body.

Some of these illustrations from the *I Ching* are helpful for us to understand why the most intensive form of radiation energy is illuminated to the dead at the first *Bardo* or the *Chikhai Bardo*. The illumination of this most intense energy in this *Bardo* presupposes the existence of the spiritual body to respond to it. The spiritual body (or the ethereal body) in this stage is purely receptive, because it does not have any active power of consciousness. Because of its pure receptivity, the spiritual body is capable of uniting itself with the pure light which comes from its own potentiality or background. Thus to be united with this pure light means to be united with his true Self, which is none other than the background of the self. Since the unity of the Self and the self, the conscious and the unconscious, or the background and foreground, in man is the ultimate goal of his existence, the moment of death which makes this possible is extremely important. The significance of this moment for the dying person is well expressed by Carl Jung. He said:

The supreme vision comes not at the end of the *Bardo*, but right at the beginning, in the moment of death; what happens afterward is an ever-deepening descent into illusion and obstruction, down to the ultimate degradation of new physical birth. The spiritual climax is reached at the moment when life ends. [38]

NOTES AND REFERENCES

[1] Elisabeth Kübler-Ross, *On Death and Dying* (New York: Macmillan Company, 1969), pp. 99ff.

[2] Cicely Saunders, The Moment of Truth," in *Death and Dying*, Ed. by Leonard Pearson (Cleveland: The Press of Case Western Reserve University, 1969), p. 59.

[3] *The Tibetan Book of the Dead*, Ed. by W. Y. Evans-Wentz (Oxford: Oxford University Press, 1960), p. 92, note 4.

[4] *Ibid.*

[5] Robert Kastenbaum, "Psychological Death," in *Death and Dying*, p. 9.

[6] *Ibid.*, p. 6.

[7] *The Tibetan Book of the Dead*, p. 93.

[8] *Ibid.*

[9] Robert Kastenbaum, *op. cit.*, p. 8.

[10] Elisabeth Kübler-Ross, *op. cit.*, pp. 246-247.

[11] C. Saunders, *op. cit.*, p. 78.

[12] *The Tibetan Book of the Dead*, p. xviii.

[13] *Bhagavad-Gita*, VIII, 6.

[14] *The Tibetan Book of the Dead*, p. xv.

[15] C. Saunders, *op. cit.*, p. 78.

[16] *The Tibetan Book of the Dead*, p. 91.

[17] Sir John Woodroffe, "Foreword," *The Tibetan Book of the Dead*, p. lxxi.

[18] *The Tibetan Book of the Dead*, p. 89, note 3.

[19] *Ibid.*, p. 91.

[20] *The Tibetan Book of the Dead*, p. 90.

[21] *Ibid.*, p. 87.

[22] *Ibid.*, p. xv.

[23] *Ibid.*, p. 98, note 3.

[24] Short and energetic radiation is invisible and colorless or formless to our eyes. The energy of electromagnetic radiation is proportional to its frequency and inversely proportional to its wavelength. See Richard A. Goldsby, *Cells and Energy* (New York: Macmillan, 1967), pp. 66-67.

[25] *The Tibetan Book of the Dead*. p. 161, note 3.

[26] For the symbol of this hexagram see Chap. III (p. 27).

[27] For the symbol of hexagram *K'un* see Chap. III (p. 27).

[28] For the symbol of hexagram *Fu* see Chap. III (p. 25).

[29] *The Tibetan Book of the Dead*, p. 92, note 4.

[30] For the symbol of this hexagram see Chap. III (p. 25).

[31] Richard A. Goldsby, *op. cit.*, p. 67.

[32] Cf. J. Y. Lee, *The Principle of Changes*, pp. 67ff.

[33] For the symbol of *Kuai* see Chap. III (p. 25).

[34] For the symbol of *Ch'ien* see Chap. III (p. 25).

[35] For the symbol of *Kou* see Chap. III (p. 27).

[36] For the symbol of *Tun* see Chap. III (p. 27).

[37] *The Tibetan Book of the Dead*, pp. 95-96.

[38] Carl Jung, "Psychological Commentary," in *The Tibetan Book of the Dead*, p. li.

7 | *The Real Experience of Death*

The Phenomena of the *Chönyid Bardo*

According to the *Bardo Thödol*, the real experience of death does not come to the dead until he is awakened from the "swoon", which marks the initial and the most important stage of death. If the dead is unable to liberate himself by recognizing the Clear Light of the Void, which comes to him at the very moment of death, he is to be led to the *Chönyid Bardo*, which is "the *Bardo* of the experiencing of reality." [1] In this stage the dead is recovered from the "swoon" and begins to recognize that he is dead. This death-consciousness is somewhat analogous with the empirical consciousness. The consciousness is relative to the ethereal body, while the empirical consciousness is dependent on the physical body. The former is quite similar to the consciousness of a dreamer. Thus sGam-po-pa states:

The intermediate state of birth-death has to be attuned to the intermediate state of dreaming, and the latter must be attuned to the former. [2]

As Woodroffe said:

Just as a dream reproduces waking experiences, so in the after-death state a man who was wont to drink and smoke imagines that he still does so. We have here to deal with "dream-whisky" and "dream-cigars" which, though imaginary, are, for the dreamer, as real as the substances he drank and smoked in his waking state. [3]

When the dead is awakened from the "swoon", he is transformed to the ethereal body with the *karmic* propensities. Thus the text of the *Bardo Thödol* says,

While on the second stage of the *Bardo*, one's body is of the nature of that called the shining illusory-body. [4]

This pure and shining illusory body or the spiritual body possesses the consciousness-principle because of the *karmic* propensities. Thus in this stage of death the *karmic* illusions begin to appear in visions and images which the dead can see in this *Bardo* period. They can be compared with the movie films which have recorded the previous life of the dead. In the *Chikhai Bardo* the *karmic* impressions have not appeared. Thus the Clear Light of the Void could shine directly to the dead. However, in the *Chönyid Bardo* the dead no longer sees the light by itself. He has to see it through his own *karmic* impressions or his movie films. Because he has to see the light through those movie films, he has to see the visions and images of his own life. However, the dead sees the movie films of his experience in a reverse order. Let us suppose that the very moment of his death marks the end of his film. Instead of the film rewinding before his seeing it, the dead begins to see it at the same place where the film ended. Thus the dead in this *Bardo* sees the visions of his own death first. The text of the *Bardo Thödol*, Part II, begins with the visions of his own body and the relatives and his friends who are weeping and wailing for his death:

About this time the deceased can see that the share of food is being set aside, that the body is being stripped of its garments, that the place of the sleeping-rug is being swept; can hear all the weeping and wailing of his friends and relatives, and although he can see them and can hear them calling upon him, they cannot hear him calling upon them, so he goeth away displeased.[5]

The death-experience begins with death and ends with birth or rebirth. Thus the journey of *Bardo* is a backward movement or inverse process of the life experience. As the *Bardo Thödol* says,

the *Bardo* [during the experiencing] of Reality; the *Bardo* of the inverse process of *sangsāric* existence.[6]

Because of its inverse process which has already begun with the *Chönyid Bardo*, the process of reincarnation has already taken place with the appearance of *karmic* impressions. However, the definite trend toward the reincarnation of the dead takes place at the third *Bardo* or the *Sidpa Bardo*. Thus it is often called the *Bardo* of Reincarnation.

Before we explain in detail some of the apparent visions and images the dead visualizes in the *Chönyid Bardo*, let us consider the metaphysical implication as to the inverse process of *Bardo* experience. Why does the dead see the movie film of his own life in an inverse order? In order to answer this question, we must come back to the principle of changes in the *I Ching*. According to this book, everything changes. The living as well as the dead are no exception to the principle and power of change. What makes the change possible is none other than the interplay of yin and yang. The process of this interplay is well explained in the diagram known as *T'ai Chi T'u*, or the Diagram of the Supreme Ultimate, which explains the origins of the principle of changes and the process of cosmic evolution.[7] In the diagram the dark portion represents yin and the light represents yang. When yin increases to its maximum degree, it has to reverse itself toward its minimum degree. At the same time, when yang increases to its maximum degree, it also has to revert itself toward the minimum degree again. In this kind of mutual relationship, we can say that the increase of yin is also the decrease of yang and the increase of yang is the decrease of yin. They are inversely proportional. When this principle of change is applied to life and death, we see the similar relationship. Yang represents life and yin represents death. When yang or life is at its minimum degree, yin or death begins to grow toward its minimum degree. In other words, the minimum degree of life and the maximum degree of death are one. That is why we have indicated that the very moment of its occurrence death occupies the deepest realm of unconsciousness. In this very moment of death, both life and death are one. From this same place both life and death move. Life begins to expand, and death begins to contract. Here we see clearly that the movement of death is reversed. Anything that has been expanded to its maximum degree has to retreat to its minimum degree. Since death has reached its maximum at the very moment of death, that is, at the *Chikhai Bardo*, it ought to retreat. Thus, in the second stage of death, that is, in the *Chönyid Bardo*, the dead experiences the reverse movement of his life experience. That is why Lao Tzu said, "As soon as things flourish, they return again to their roots." [8] The reverse movement is the way of *Tao*, the principle of changes. Because of this principle of changes which affect both the living and the dead, the dead sees his own life experience in a reverse order.

Let us now consider how the movie film of life experience is seen by the dead in an inverse order. Let us imagine a film-projector showing coloured film, throwing pictures and sounds on a screen. [9] The following diagram may be helpful in understanding the visions and sound that the dead can see and hear.

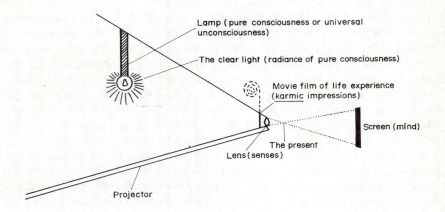

Lamp (pure consciousness or universal unconsciousness)

The clear light (radiance of pure consciousness)

Movie film of life experience (karmic impressions)

Screen (mind)

The present

Lens (senses)

Projector

From the diagram we see that the dead cannot see the Clear Light of the Void in the second stage of death. He sees the light through *karmic* impressions, which are recorded in the movie film. However, before the *karmic* impressions appear, the Clear Light comes directly to the dead without video tape or *karmic* impressions. Thus the light is void. However, in the *Chönyid Bardo* the same Clear Light is seen through *karmic* impressions or movie film. Thus in this period the dead sees the various visions and sounds coming from the film, even though the Clear Light is still shining as usual. Because the Light comes to the dead indirectly through the movie film, it is *karmically* conditioned. Just as we see only colored pictures and sounds when we look on the screen of the movie projector, the dead also sees the visions and images in different colors and sounds in different tones. It is then like the dream-state, where the dreamer sees visions and hears the sounds of his own. Just as the dreamer sees visions which are quite different from those which have been seen in life, the dead also sees the visions of different colors which are quite different from those which he has experienced in life. In other words, the movie film does not reproduce his life experience in the same manner in which he has experienced life. Why do the visions and sounds to the dead appear differently from the forms of life experience?

Even though the forms of visions and sounds are quite different in the *Bardo*, they are the same things which the dead has experienced in life. Just as the things which we see and hear are quite different when we see and hear them through a delicate machine like a radiospectrometer, the things that the dead experienced in life are seen differently in his death. Since the dead does not have the physical body but rather the astral body, he cannot see and hear in the same manner as he had done in life. For example, in the astral world the differentiation between water and ice is not possible. Even though there are various phenomenal differentiations to the senses of the physical body, there are several diffused images of astral light which are available to the senses of the astral body of the dead. The dead can see only the various forms of natural light of nature. Thus, Evans-Wentz said,

Only the natural light of nature (refered to by medieval alchemists and mystics as the "astral light") is to be seen in the after-death state; and this "astral light" is said to be universally diffused throughout the ether, like an earth twilight, yet quite bright enough for the eyes of the ethereally constituted beings in the *Bardo*.[10]

Thus the *sangsāric* experience in various forms has to be deduced to the *Bardo* experience in astral forms. The manifestations of the astral world to the dead are different in visions and forms from those of the physical world, but they are essentially the same. This resembles the reductive process of common phenomena to certain codes or archetypes. Since the *Bardo* senses can see and hear certain patterns and colors only, all the *sangsāric* experiences are to be coded into certain colors, patterns, and tones that the astral senses can perceive. Thus the movie film which is to be projected before the dead conveys those symbols which the *Bardo* senses can perceive. What, then, are the coded symbols or patterns which the dead can perceive with his astral senses? How is life experience coded into the movie film?

Let me attempt to answer the latter first. What is experienced in life is not recorded in the movie film directly. In other words, unless the experience itself becomes a part of one's real self, it is not to be recorded. That is to say, what is recorded in the movie film which is to be projected in the *Bardo* is none other than the content of himself. Thus the visions and images which the dead sees are none other than the reflections of his true self. When a man dies, he can see himself as he is. As the dead sees himself truly, he recognizes that he has two selves. In other words, the movie film projects two different pictures of himself. One picture of him deals with the empirical self, which is the byproduct of his empirical life. Another picture of him deals with the background of his empirical self, that is, the archetypal Self or the Cosmic Consciousness. These two selves are projected to the dead simultaneously. The empirical self appears in the forms of dull light, while the cosmic or archetypal Self appears in the images of bright and dazzling light. The former deals with the *conscious*, while the latter with the *unconscious*. As Woodroffe said:

The deceased being thus in the world of duality, we find that from this point onwards there is a double parallel presentation to his consciousness. There is firstly a *Nirvānic* line, comprising the Five *Dhyāni* Buddhas of the *Sambhoga-Kayā* symbolized by various dazzling colors, with certain Divinities, peaceful and wrathful, emanating from them; and secondly, a *Sangsāric* line, consisting of the Six *Lokas*. [11]

The appearance of double presentation signifies the co-existence of the archetypal Self with the empirical self. Thus the movie film contains both the archetypal Self and the empirical self, for both of them are inseparable.

The consciousness-principle in the ethereal body apprehends six distinctive colors of radiance coming from both the archetypal Self and the empirical self. They are white, blue, yellow, red, green, and black. The first five are primary colors applicable to both radiances of the archetypal Self and the empirical self. The black color is combined with the colored radiances of the empirical self and creates the dull hues. The colored radiances from the archetypal Self are shining and bright, while those from the empirical self are dull and dim. Moreover, these radiances appear to the dead in certain forms or visions, which may have to do with the archetypes of ideas that the dead had experienced. Carl Jung points out clearly that the visions of deities which the dead visualizes are none other than the archetypal fantasy-forms, which appear in the dream-state, in psychosis, and in the *Bardo*.

They are eternally inherited forms and ideas which have at first no specific content. Their specific content only appears in the course of the individual's life, when personal experience is taken up in precisely these forms. [12]

These archetypal forms which do not have any specific content in the beginning are given different contents by the different traditions of belief. For example, the Buddhist may give Buddhist content to these archetypes, while the Christian may give Christian content to them. These archetypal forms are universal, but their contents will vary according to different traditions. Since the *Bardo Thödol* belongs to the Buddhist tradition, it describes the Buddhist contents of archetypal ideas. We can examine in detail the archetypal visions appearing to the dead in the *Chönyid Bardo*.

According to the *Bardo Thödol*, the *Chönyid Bardo* lasts fourteen days altogether. It begins with the awakening of death-consciousness after about three or four days of "swoon". Thus it reads on the first day of *Chönyid Bardo* as follows:

O nobly-born, thou hast been in a "swoon" during the last three and one-half days. As soon as thou are recovered from this "swoon", thou wilt have the thought, "What hath happened!" [13]

As soon as he is recovered from the "swoon", he sees the white radiance coming from the Central Realm of Cosmic Buddha, the Bhagavān Vairochana, who is embraced by the Mother of the Space of Heaven. Here, the Vairochana represents the male principle or yang of the universe, while the Mother of the Space of Heaven represents the female principle or yin of the universe. In other words, they represent the primordial principles of yin and yang, the hexagram *Ch'ien* and *K'un* in the *I Ching*.[14] The combination of these two primordial principles emanates the bright and shining radiance in white. Along with this shining and dazzling light there also appears the dull white light of the *devas*. In the second day, the blue radiance comes from the Eastern Realm of Pre-eminent Happiness, the Bhagavān Akshobhya, who is embraced by the Mother Māmaki. At the same time the dead sees the dull, smoke-colored light from hell. On the third day the shining yellow light comes from the Southern Realm of Cosmic Buddha, the Bhagavān Ratna-Sambhava, who is embraced by the Divine Mother Sangyay-Chanma. Side by side with it, the dull yellow light from the human world comes to him. On the fourth day the dead sees the red light coming from the Western Realm of Happiness, the Bhagavān Buddha Amitabha, who is accompanied by the Divine Mother Gökarmo. Along with this bright and shining light the dull red light comes to him from the *Preta-loka*, the world of unhappy ghosts. On the fifth day the green light comes to the dead from the Northern Realm of Successful Performance of Best Actions, the Bhagavān Buddha Amogha-Siddhi, who is accompanied by the Divine Mother, the Faithful

Dölma. Along with it, a light of dull green color comes to him from the *Asura-loka*, the world of titans. During the first five days of the *Chönyid Bardo* the dead sees the five different colors proceeding separately.

The visions of deities which the dead sees are peaceful ones. Each color of light represents a different order of Dhyāni Buddhas. However, on the sixth day all of them appear to the dead at the same time. The text says,

> Thereupon all the Divine Fathers-Mothers of the Five Orders of [Dhyāni Buddhas] with their attendants will come to shine upon one simultaneously. At the same time, the lights proceeding from the Six *Lokas* will likewise come to shine upon one simultaneously.[15]

The lights of different colors no longer come separately one by one. Both bright and dull lights come to him altogether at once. Thus it is said,

> O nobly born, along with the radiances of Wisdom, the impure illusory lights of the Six *Lokas* will also come to shine ... a dull white light from the *devas*, a dull green light from the *asuras*, a dull yellow light from human beings, a dull blue light from the brutes, a dull reddish light from the *pretas*, and a dull smoke-colored light from Hell. These six thus will come to shine ....[16]

Here, we notice that the dull smoke-colored light or dark light from the Hell is added on the sixth day. Thus the light paths of Five Orders of Wisdom and six *lokas* are simultaneously shining to the dead. The dawning of the peaceful deities is to end at the seventh day. On this last day of the dawning of the peaceful deities, these deities appear to the dead as the Knowledge-Holding Deities. There are five Knowledge-Holding Deities, because of the five light paths of Dhyāni Buddha. Along with these five deities, a dull blue light from the brute world comes to him. However, at this time the dead not only sees the colored lights but hears the sounds. It is said,

> Within those radiances, the natural sound of the Truth will reverberate like a thousand thunders. The sound will come with a rolling reverberation, amidst which will be heard, "Slay! Slay!" and awe-inspiring *mantras*.[17]

During these seven days the dead is to be liberated if he can recognize the bright and shining radiances and unite with them. If the dead is not liberated by the seventh day, he has to go through the next stage of *Chönyid Bardo* which begins on the eighth day.

From the eighth to the fourteenth day is known as the time of the dawning of the wrathful deities. We see the sacred "seven" number is to be repeated again in this period. The former seven days will repeat in this second stage of the *Chönyid Bardo* appearing in different forms of visions and images. The peaceful deities become the wrathful ones. As it is said,

> After the cessation [of the dawning] of the Peaceful and the Knowledge-Holding Deities, who come to welcome one, the fifty-eight flame-enhaloed, wrathful, blood-drinking deities come to dawn, who are only the former Peaceful Deities in changed aspect — according to the place [or psychic-center of the *Bardo* body of the deceased whence they proceed]; nevertheless, they will not resemble them.[18]

We will see that the eighth day corresponds to the first day. However, this time the dead is far away from the center of Pure Light. Thus he sees more colors in less intense light. On the eighth day the Bhagavān Vairochana and His counterpart, which appeared on the first day, reappears as the Great Glorious Buddha-Heruka, who is embodied by the Mother Buddha-Krotishaurima. These blood-drinking deities consist of three heads, six hands, and four feet. They are the most fearful images which scare the dead off. Moreover, they also create the palatal sound like the crackling sound and a rumbling sound as loud as thunder.

On the ninth day the dead sees the changed form of Bhagavān Vajra-Sattva, who is accompanied with his counterpart, appeared on the second day. The Bhagavān Vajra-Sattva is changed to the blood-drinking deity of the Bhagavān Vajra-Heruka, who is embraced by the Mother Vaira-Krotichaurima. On the tenth day the Father-Mother Bhagavān Ratna-Sambhava, who appeared on the third day, will come to the dead as the blood-drinking and wrathful deity known as Ratna-Heruka along with the Mother Ratna-Krotishaurima. On the eleventh day the dead sees the blood-drinking Lotus Order known as the Bhagavān Padma-Heruka, embraced by the Mother Padma-Krotishaurima, who appeared as the Father-Mother Bhagavān Amitābha on the fourth day. On the twelfth day the Father-Mother Bhagavān Amogha-Siddhi, which appeared to the dead on the fifth day, changes to the wrathful deities of the Karmic Order, known as Karma-Heruka with the Mother Karma-Krotishaurima. On the thirteenth day all the five blood-drinking orders of deities appear to the dead simultaneously. They are the changed forms of the Five Orders of Deities who appeared to him on the sixth day. There appear the eight directions of light which are surrounded by the five blood-drinking deities. The fourteenth day or the last day of the *Chönyid Bardo* corresponds to the seventh day. The Knowledge-Holding Deities, which appeared on the seventh day, will appear in the changed forms on the fourteenth day. They change to different forms of Goddesses who hold various images. Some of them are the White Tiger-Headed God-Holding Goddess, the Yellow Sow-Headed Noose-Holding Goddess, the Lion-Headed Iron-Chain-Holding Goddess, and the Green Serpent-Headed Bell-Holding Goddess. Altogether there are twenty-eight Goddesses in the forms of the wrathful deities, which are none other than the reappearances of the Knowledge-Holding Deities. Both the peaceful deities appeared on the first seven days and the wrathful deities appeared on the last seven days come from the same Dharma-Kāya.

O nobly-born, the Peaceful Deities emanate from the Voidness of the Dharma-Kāya; recognize them. From the Radiance of the Dharma-Kāya emanate the Wrathful Deities; recognize them.[19]

Thus the visions and sounds of the first seven days reappear in their changed forms on the second seven days of the *Chönyid Bardo*. If the dead does not realize the visions of deities in either peaceful or wrathful forms as the emanating energy expressions of his own archetypal Self, he cannot be liberated from the chain of birth and death. Thus he has to come to the last *Bardo*, the *Sidpa Bardo*, to continue the rest of his *Bardo* journey until he is born again. As soon as the dead reaches the gate of the *Sidpa Bardo* he is almost incapable of liberation. He should aim at the higher rebirth to life.

For those who are not familiar with the Buddhist (especially Tantric) teachings, it is rather meaningless and confusing to describe various forms of divine visions and their consorts and door-keepers, and so forth. For those who are Christians, those visions may appear to them as Christian angels and saints. The contents of archetypes vary according to different traditions and orientations. Thus our primary interest in examining the various visions and sounds the dead sees in the *Chönyid Bardo* does not deal with the contents but with the archetypes which do not have contents in themselves. What we know from the descriptions we have made during the fourteen days of the *Bardo* experience can be best described in terms of psychic hallucinations. That is why Carl Jung calls the *Chönyid* state as "equivalent to a deliberately induced psychosis." [20] There is a striking similarity between the experience of *Chönyid Bardo* and that of the psychedelic state. One of the classic attempts to test the possibility of experiencing the *Chönyid Bardo* was Aldous Huxley, who made use of mescaline as means of stimulation. While he was in the mescaline experiment, his wife asked him:

Would you be able to fix your attention on what *The Tibetan Book of the Dead* calls the Clear Light?

Then Huxley answered:

Perhaps I could — but only if there were somebody there to tell me about the Clear Light. One couldn't do it by oneself. That's the point, I suppose, of the Tibetan ritual — someone sitting there all the time telling you what's what.

He then later added:

What those Buddhist monks did for the dying and the dead, might not the modern psychiatrist do for the insane? [21]

Huxley explained his experience when he was under the influence of mescaline. He had the sense of transformation, beatific vision, the infinite mind, the void and many wonderful visions which the *Bardo Thödol* attempts to describe. LSD seems to produce the similar experience to that which the mescaline does, even though "LSD has relatively long time-course (about eight hours), as does mescaline." [22] It creates the structured pseudo-hallucinations consisting of dream-like sequences of panoramic visions, tranquil scenes, or imagined horrors. Various images and visions as well as colors become so real that one can feel he can almost taste and touch them. He feels his oneness with the universe or Nirvana when he is under the influence of LSD. Moreover, sounds can be experienced either visually or as bodily vibrations or sensations. Some of these descriptive phenomena under the influence of psychedelic drugs are very much similar to what the *Bardo Thödol* describes in the *Chönyid Bardo*. The similarity between these two experiences helps us to see the deeper implications than mere visions and sounds in the *Bardo* journey. The apparitional visions the dead could visualize in the *Chönyid Bardo* have their origin in psychic or mental impulses.

The peaceful deities which appear for the first seven days during the *Chönyid Bardo* are none other than the personified forms of the highest human sentiments proceeding from the psychic heart of the ethereal body. They are not external to the dead but expressions of his own feelings about his relatives and friends who are left behind him. Everything the dead has seen is the radiance of his own nature. Thus it is said,

Be not daunted thereby, nor terrified, nor awed. That is the radiance of thine own true nature. Recognize it. [23]

The Clear Light which appears in the personified forms of various peaceful deities proceeds from the heart-center of the archetypal Self. On the other hand, the dull light proceeds from the heart-impulses of his empirical self. Thus the peaceful visions are the personifications of the feelings proceeding from the heart of the dead. On the other hand, the wrathful deities which are reappearances of the peaceful deities are the personifications of the reasonings coming from the brain impulses. The impulses from the heart-center of the dead are transformed into the impulses of reasoning from the brain-center. As Evans-Wentz said,

Just as impulses arising in the heart-center may transform themselves into the reasonings of the brain-center, so the Wrathful Deities are the Peaceful Deities in a changed aspect. [24]

The peaceful deities which have appeared from the various realms of heaven are the hallucinatory visions coming from the different parts of his heart-centers. They reappear from the eighth to the fourteenth day as the wrathful deities from the brain-center. Thus the wrathful deities which seem to come from many different directions of the world are, in reality, the hallucinatory embodiments of different realms of the brain-center. The five main wrathful deities, for example, come from the five different quarters of the brain-center of the one who sees them in the last seven days of *Chönyid Bardo*. That is why it is said,

At this time when the Fifty-eight Blood-Drinking Deities emanating from thine own brain come to shine upon thee, if thou knowest them to be the radiances of thine own intellect, thou wilt merge, in the state of atonement, into the body of the Blood-Drinking Ones there and then, and obtain Buddhahood. [25]

Since everything that the dead experiences comes from his own psychic and mental thought-form, the experience of the *Chönyid Bardo* is not really different from a peculiar form of psychic phenomena. That is why, as Carl Jung said, the *Chönyid* state is quite similar to deliberately induced psychosis. The following text describes clearly the similarity of suffering and tormenting experience between the deliberately induced psychosis and the *Chönyid* state:

Then [one of the Executive Furies of] the Lord of Death will place round thy neck a rope and drag thee along; he will cut off thy hand, extract thy heart, pull out thy intestines, lick up thy brain, drink thy blood, eat thy flesh, and gnaw thy bones; but thou wilt be incapable of dying. Although thy body be hacked to pieces, it will revive again. The repeated hacking will cause intense pain and torture . . . Thy body being a mental body is incapable of dying even though beheaded and quartered. In reality, thy body is of the nature of voidness; thou needst not be afraid. The Lord of Death are thine own hallucinations. [26]

Finally, we may question why the experience of the *Chönyid Bardo* is similar to that of the drug-induced psychosis. If the *Bardo Thödol* is, as Saher describes,

the first record we have of a *purely philosophical* attempt at a coldly scientific, reasoned analysis of the after-death state uncontaminated by guesswork, [27]

we may be able to explain why the experience of the after-death state is similar to that of deliberately induced psychosis. The similarity of their experiences presupposes the similarity of the circumstances which make those experiences possible. In other words, the mental condition under the influence of a drug like LSD must be similar to the *Bardo* mentality. According to the *Bardo Thödol*, death is not the extinction of the conscious self but the transformation of it into the *Bardo* body.

The *Bardo* body, formed of matter in an invisible or ethereal-like state, is an exact duplicate of the human body, from which it is separated in the process of death. Retained in the *Bardo* body are the consciousness-principle and the psychic nerve-system (the counterpart, for the psychic or *Bardo* body, of the physical nerve-system of the human body). [28]

This *Bardo* mentality, then, is the counterpart of the physical mentality. The former is dominated by the power of unconsciousness, the latter by the power of empirical consciousness. In other words, the *Bardo* mentality is no longer under the domination of the power of empirical consciousness, even though it still possesses the consciousness-principle and the psychic nerve-system. It is, then, the liberation of the mind from the power of empirical consciousness which attempts to focus the mind towards the particularization of things. To say it in another way, the power of the empirical self is no longer active when man is dead. The dead is free from the restriction of the empirical self, even though he has to visualize its manifestations in the forms of hallucinatory visions in the *Bardo* journey. The complete revelation of his archetypal Self is possible at death. Thus the mental condition of the *Bardo* body is best described in terms of the nullification of empirical conscious-activities. We also see similar phenomena of the mental condition under the influence of the psychedelic drugs such as LSD and mescaline. One of the most important functions of LSD, for example, is to disrupt the conditioned reflexes, which are based on the activities of empirical consciousness. [29] LSD impairs accuracy of discrimination and reduces the functional efficiency of the brain. In other words, the psychedelic drugs can temporarily stop the power of the empirical consciousness, so that the inner power of the archetypal Self can be active. Thus the psychedelic drugs can create the similar condition of the *Bardo* mentality. As long as the mental condition of the deliberately induced psychosis is similar to that of the *Bardo* body, it is reasonable to believe that the experience of the *Chönyid Bardo* has some similarity with the experience of the drug-induced state. We see, therefore, why Carl Jung compares the *Chönyid Bardo* with deliberately induced psychosis.

NOTES AND REFERENCES

[1] *The Tibetan Book of the Dead*, compiled and edited by W. E. Evans-Wentz (New York: Oxford University Press, 1960), pp. 101ff.

[2] sGam-po-pa, *The Collected Works of sGam-po-pa*, xvii, 46; quoted in *The Life and Teaching of Naropa*, Trans. by H. Guenther (Oxford University Press, 1963), p. 246.

[3] John Woodroffe, "Foreword," in *The Tibetan Book of the Dead*, p. lxxv.

[4] *The Tibetan Book of the Dead*, p. 100.

[5] *The Tibetan Book of Dead*, p. 101-102.

[6] *Ibid.*, p. 102.

[7] J. Y. Lee, *The Principle of Changes: Understanding the I Ching* (New Hyde Park: University Books, 1971), p. 46.

[8] *Tao Te Ching*, Chap. 16 (my own translation).

[9] P. J. Saher attempts to illustrate the visions which the dead visualize through the use of slides. Slides are inadequate to illustrate it, because they do not produce sounds. It is said, "At that time, sounds, lights, and rays — all three — are experienced." (*Tibetan Book of the Dead*, p. 102). Thus it is better to use the movie film, which produces both sounds and pictures, to illustrate the visions and sounds that the dead hears. See Saher, *Eastern Wisdom and Western Thought* (London: George Allen and Unwin, 1969), p. 249.

[10] *The Tibetan Book of the Dead*, p. 161, note 3.

[11] John Woodroffe, "Foreword" in *The Tibetan Book of the Dead*, p. lxxvii.

[12] Carl Jung, "Psychological Commentary," in *The Tibetan Book of the Dead*, p. xliv.

[13] *The Tibetan Book of the Dead*, p. 105.

[14] J. Y. Lee, *The Principle of Changes*, p. 141.

[15] *The Tibetan Book of the Dead*, p. 118.

[16] *Ibid.*, p. 124.

[17] *The Tibetan Book of the Dead*, p. 129.

[18] *The Tibetan Book of the Dead*, p. 131.

[19] *The Tibetan Book of the Dead*, p. 146.

[20] Carl Jung, "Psychological Commentary," in *The Tibetan Book of the Dead*, p. xlvi.

[21] See A. Huxley, *The Doors of Perception* (New York: Harper and Row, 1954), pp. 57-58; cf. P. J. Saher, *op. cit.*, p. 166.

[22] Jerome Levine, "LSD — A Clinical Overview," in *Drugs and the Brain*, Ed. by Perry Black (Baltimore: The Johns Hopkins Press, 1969), p. 301.

23 *The Tibetan Book of the Dead*, p. 104.

24 *Ibid.*, p. 31.

25 *Ibid.*, pp. 166-67.

26 *The Tibetan Book of the Dead*, pp. 166-67.

27 Saher, *op. cit.*, p. 248.

28 *The Tibetan Book of the Dead*, p. 92, note 4.

29 Perry Black and others, "Behavioral Effects of LSD in Subhuman Primates," in *Drugs and the Brain*, Ed. by Perry Black (Baltimore: The Johns Hopkins Press, 1969), p. 292.

8 | The Process of Reincarnation

The Phenomena of *Sidpa Bardo*

The problem of reincarnation seems to have become a vital issue in the West in our time. Some contemporary writers are examining the possibility of reincarnation of souls. In *Look* magazine, Eugene Kinkead seems to conclude that some of the actual case studies support the theory of reincarnation.[1] Leslie D. Weatherhead, who was the minister of the City Temple, London for 25 years, expresses his view of reincarnation. He says:

> I could give you case after case of the most amazing things that have happened for which I can't find any other explanation than that of reincarnation. For instance, Sir William Hamilton at thirteen could speak thirteen languages. Though just a boy, he wrote a letter to the Persian ambassador. The diplomat read it and then said, "Look, this is not modern Persian; this is ancient script of the Persian language which passed out of use years ago." Now how on earth did this boy know ancient Persian?[2]

He gives many examples such as the above and supports the theory of reincarnation as a part of Christian tradition. When he was asked by Dr. Maltby about the Christian belief as to the theory of reincarnation, he said,

> I don't see anything in this theory which contradicts the Christian position. In our Lord's time it was part of the accepted beliefs of everybody.[3]

As Weatherhead said, the concept of reincarnation was accepted in the time of the New Testament. There are many places in the Gospels where the concept of reincarnation is alluded to. One of the best known passages in the Gospels deals with Jesus' question to his disciples about His own image. He asked them, "Who do men say that I am?" They answered, "Some say John the Baptist; some Elijah; and others Jeremiah or one of the prophets." (Matthew 16:13, 14.) Jesus did not say that they were speaking nonsense, because the idea of reincarnation was accepted. However, the theory of reincarnation was rejected as a part of the Church's doctrines at the Council of Constantinople in 533 A.D. Since that time, the Church has denounced the idea of reincarnation. Following the teachings of the Church, the dominant trend of the West has been the rejection of reincarnation. The idea of reincarnation has often been thought to be alien to the Christian faith and to be part of Eastern religions. However, in recent times more and more people in the West take the idea of reincarnation seriously.

There are two specific reasons why the West has rejected the idea of reincarnation. One of them deals with the idea of time and the other with the idea of heaven and hell. The former deals with the concept of history, while the latter with the concept of salvation. In the West, both science and religion (Christianity) are interested in the linear movement of history. In other words, the main trend of Western thought is to conceive time in terms of lineal change. History has been conceived in terms of constant advancement and progress. The constant evolvement of conscious minds has been clearly evidenced in the development of scientific technology in the West. Christianity also views history in terms of the lineal movement toward the ultimate goal. The drama of the Christian Bible also has been conceived in terms of movement from promise to fulfillment or from the beginning to the end. Therefore, it is commonly understood by scholars in our time that the real distinction in thinking of the West from the East is in the lineal change of time. However, we begin to see that time cannot move straight, as it has been understood by the West. With the contemporary development of astronomical science and the general theory of relativity, the interstellar space is understood to be curved. Everything that moves along the space is seen to move in a curved path. Everything in the world changes according to the curvature of space. If we conceive time as the unit of change, the unit ought to be curved, because change takes place in the form of a circle.[4] The Euclidean notion of time and space, which extends infinitely, is no longer acceptable in the light of new developments in science. Moreover, both time and space are not independent. They are mutually interdependent and relative to the process of change.[5] We also see that the end of the world which Christianity describes is not the end only. It is also the beginning of the renewed. The end of the old heaven and earth is also the coming of the new heaven and new earth in the book of Revelation. Thus, time does not move straight from the beginning to the end but moves in a form of a circle or an ellipse because of the principle of changes. The denial of the lineal movement of time is in fact the possibility of allowing the idea of reincarnation.

The concept of hell and heaven after death became a basis for the denial of reincarnation. If there is an eternal heaven and hell where the dead go and stay forever, it is no use to speculate about the idea of reincarnation. Since there are places of eternal rest, the dead do not return to the world. The idea of eternal heaven and hell was based on the world view of that time. If we look at the world view of the New Testament, for example, it is understood in terms of three-storied buildings. Thus, Rudolf Bultmann begins his famous essay of demythologizing with the cosmology of the New Testament:

The cosmology of the New Testament is essentially mystical in character. The world is viewed as a three-storied structure, with the earth in the centre, the heaven above, and the underworld beneath. Heaven is the abode of God and of celestial beings — the angels. The underworld is hell, the place of torment. [6]

In this kind of world-view the eternal separation of heaven and earth and hell was possible. However, in our contemporary world-view it is impossible to separate heaven, earth and hell. Heaven is not the abode of the divine, and the underworld is not the place of torment and hell. This kind of spatiotemporal thinking is no longer feasible in the light of the space-time continuum. In the constant flow and change, the isolation of one place from others is unthinkable. There is no place where the process of change does not take place. In the world of process and change, the static view of heaven and hell is not possible. The denial of heaven and hell as the eternal places where the dead go, that is, the denial of the traditional view of the Euclidean space and time, is in fact the denial of any absolute claim that reincarnation is not possible. In other words, it opens the door for the possibility of the reincarnation of the dead. Thus, to deny the eternal abode of the dead is in reality to allow the possibility of reincarnation.

With these introductory remarks let us begin our investigation into the process of reincarnation. As we have already pointed out, the idea of reincarnation presupposes the concept of change which affects all things whether they are dead or living. The theory of reincarnation is feasible as long as the dead are subject to the principle of changes. Since change takes place according to the process of expansion and contraction or growth and decay, it is also the process of constant recurrences. Because of this process of recurrences, the principle of change is cyclic in character. For example, day returns again when night is gone, because it follows the principle of changes. Thus the way of change is often understood as the way of returning. The process of returning is a cycle of change. This cycle of change makes reincarnation possible. Thus everything that changes is capable of reincarnation. In this respect the word "reincarnation" is not the right word. It is rather meaningful to call it "renewal", since it is the returning of the old. Since the process of this renewal occurs in all that which is changing, man who also changes is no exception to this renewal. Man is not essentially different from plants and animals in a strict sense. He is a part of nature and a child of earth. Thus, as one of the Upanishads says, man is not really different from corn: "like corn a mortal ripens and like corn he is born again." [7] Man is subject to the very same law of changes which controls all things. This kind of law is attributed to the Creator in the books of the Old Testament Apocrypha:

Mother says, "I don't know how you appeared in my wombs; it was not I who endowed you with breath and life, I had not the shaping of your every part. It is the creator of the world, ordaining the process of man's birth and presiding over the origin of all things, who in his mercy will most surely give you back both breath and life, seeing that you now despise your own existence for the sake of his laws." [8]

Creation is certainly not a given fact but a constantly recurring phenomenon through the operation of the law of changes. In this law of changes there is a complementary relationship between the constructive and destructive processes. When the destructive process ends, the constructive process begins at the same time. When the process of death ends, the process of rebirth takes place. Therefore, the *Bardo Thödol* attempts to say that the process of reincarnation begins as soon as the dead person recovers from the sudden shock of the "swoon" period. Even though the process of reincarnation begins with the second stage of death, or the *Chönyid Bardo*, the real desire for reincarnation seems to be clearly expressed in the final stage or the *Sidpa Bardo*.

The *Sidpa Bardo*, or the intermediate state of seeking rebirth, deals with the transformation of the *Bardo* body or the astral body into the physical body. The process of this transformation from the *Bardo* body to the physical body seems to begin with the desire of the dead to possess the body. As the text of the *Bardo Thödol* says,

Thou wilt see thine own home, the attendants, relatives and the corpse, and think, "Now I am dead! What shall I do?" and being oppressed with intense sorrow, the thought will occur to thee, "O what would I not give to possess a body!" And so thinking, thou wilt be wandering hither and thither seeking a body. [9]

This desire to possess the body comes from his *karmic* illusions. Since the *karmic* illusions appear to the dead one as soon as he is recovered from the deep "swoon", the process of reincarnation begins with the *Chönyid Bardo*, or the *Bardo* of Experiencing the Reality of Death. However, when the dead is unable to be liberated from the power of *karma*, he is destined to be born again in the world. This actual process of rebirth is known in the *Sidpa Bardo*, which marks the end of the *Bardo* journey.

It has been said that ordinarily the miseries of the *Sidpa Bardo* are experienced for about twenty-two days; but, because of the determining influence of *karma*, a fixed period is not assured. [10]

The miseries of this *Bardo* seems to begin with the Judgment.

The most intensive pain and suffering of the dead are realized at the time of the Judgment. The *Bardo Thödol* describes the Lord of Death as the judge of the dead. He holds the Mirror of *Karma* to judge the sins or evil orientation in him. The dead cannot hide anything before the Mirror, "wherein every good and evil act is vividly reflected. Lying will be of no avail." [11] As soon as the Lord of Death consults the Mirror of Karma, he begins to execute upon dead the most intensive forms of pain and torture. However, his body is incapable of dying even though beheaded and hacked to pieces, because it is of the nature of voidness. Everything that happens at the Judgment is none other than his own hallucinations. The Lord of Death is not someone outside of himself but the imagination of his own superconsciousness. Thus the Judgment is to see his own self as it is. He can deceive others but cannot deceive himself. Thus in the final analysis the dead judges himself and tortures himself before the actual process of rebirth takes place. With the experience of terror and pain the dead may easily seek to get into a body to avoid the suffering. Thus the text says,

O what misery I am undergoing! Now, whatever body I am to get, I shall go and seek it. So thinking, thou wilt be going hither and thither, ceaselessly and distractedly. Then there will shine upon thee the lights of the Six *Sangsāric Lokas*. The light of that place wherein thou art to be born, through power of *karma*, will shine most prominently. [12]

The process of reincarnation is facilitated by the desire to avoid the intensive suffering and torture. However, the appearance of the lights of the six *Sangsāric Lokas*, or six regions of the world, signifies the six possible regions of reincarnation. Each region of the world is represented by a color signifying the radiance of his own sentiment or thought from the *Bardo* body. The *Bardo Thödol* illustrates further the different colors of six lights:

If thou desirest to know what those six lights are: there will shine upon thee a dull white light from the *Deva*-world, a dull green light from the *Asura*-world, a dull yellow light from the *Human*-world, a dull blue light from the *Brute*-world, a dull red light from the *Preta*-world, and a smoke-colored light from the *Hell*-world. [13]

When these six different radiances are seen, the dead may take one particular light or radiance because of his *karma*. As soon as he takes a certain color light, he is led to be born in that region which the light signifies. Thus it is said,

At that time, by the power of *karma*, thine own body will partake of the color of the light of the place wherein thou art to be born. [14]

It is then the power of *karma* which decides the destiny of reincarnation. Thus let us take a moment to examine the nature of *karma* before we come to discuss the actual phenomena of the rebirth process.

The word '*karma*' has been so widely used in the East that it is almost necessary to define what we mean by it. To understand *karma* in relation to the doctrine of reincarnation, we must not think of it in terms of an impersonal law of cause and effect only. It also has a profound implication for the formation of personality. Thus, Radhakrishnan said,

The theory of *karma* recognizes the rule of law not only in outward nature, but also in the world of mind and morals. [15]

Because it has to do with the mind and morals of people, it is the basis of personality formation. It is the background of their germinal character or the archetype of personality. Thus *karma* is to be understood as the background of personality formation. Carl Jung calls it a psychic heredity:

Hence we may cautiously accept the idea of *karma* only if we understand it as psychic heredity in the very widest sense of the word. Psychic heredity does exist — that is to say, there is inheritance of psychic characteristics such as predisposition to disease, traits of character, special gifts, and so forth. [16]

However, *karma* is not identical with psychic heredity. Rather the former is the foundation of the latter. The idea of *karma* as psychic heredity signifies that one's psychic origin may go back to the beginning of his human origin. In other words, the sum of tendencies to act in a certain way, which we may call the germinal character, may have a long history of evolvement in the past.

So we may justly say that this "character" — this moral and intellectual essence of a man — does veritably pass over from one fleshly tabernacle to another, and does really transmigrate from generation to generation. In the new-born infant, the character of the stock lies latent, and the Ego is little more than a bundle of potentialities. [17]

This basic inclination to act in a certain way is inherited through the line of ancestry for many millions of years since life first appeared on the earth. This tendency or *karma*, the foundation of characteristic formation, is known as the basis of an archetypal form which becomes the background of actual character. According to the *I Ching* or the Book of Changes, there are 64 different archetypes. [18] Each archetype is based on *karma*, the germinal tendency to develop into a certain character. Just as the 64 archetypes in the *I Ching* represent the microcosms of the total universe, these *karmas* can represent the basic inclinations of all things in the universe. Therefore, in a final analysis all forms of rebirth whether the living or the non-living creatures in the world are carried out by the *karmas*. Through *karmas* the archetypal forms are inherited from generation to generation without their contents, but they receive them as they are manifested in the world. That is why *karma* becomes the background of reincarnation. Reincarnation is then none other than the manifestation of karma, the archetype of characteristic formation.

The idea of *karma* as the germinal inclination which is inherent from generation to generation helps us to understand the basis for the rebirth process. It is then the *karma* which arouses the dead to seek the physical body. However, the selection of the body is dependent on the basic inclination of desire, that is, the power of *karma*. If the dead person has an evil inclination, he may seek the evil body. If he has a good inclination to act, he may seek to be reincarnated in the good world. As we said, there are the six worlds of *sangsāric* existence which are correlated to six colored lights. When these worlds of existence appear to the dead in the forms of different colored lights, he will select a certain colored light because of his basic inclination.

The correlation between *karma* and a certain colored light is a key to the selection of the womb-door. In other words, these six levels of existence correspond to six different forms of *karma*. We can illustrate the correlation between the levels of existence and the types of *karma* through the use of a hexagram. Let us draw the first hexagram, *Ch'ien* or Creativity, and examine how the level of existence is correlated

```
———————————— 6
———————————— 5
———————————— 4
———————————— 3
———————————— 2
———————————— 1
```

with the types of work. As we see from the diagram, the hexagram has six different levels of existence. The first line is regarded as the lowest, and the sixth line as the highest in position. The six levels of existence in the hexagram are in hierarchical order. If we suppose that the lines in the hexagram represent the levels of the *sangsāric* existence, the lowest line, that is, line 1, represents the hell world, while the upper level represents the god world. When the dead person confronts these different planes of existence in the forms of different colored radiance, he is attracted to a certain colored light which represents his *karma* If the dead has the pious *karma* or pious inclination to act, he may be attracted by the upper level of existence. On the other hand, if the dead has the impure desire, he may be attracted by the lower level of existence. In these ways the levels of existence and kinds of *karma* are correlated. That is why the choice of the womb-door is almost entirely dependent upon the type of *karma* the dead possesses. It is then the *karma*, the inclination to act in a certain way, which is in a final sense responsible for the selection of the physical body.

When the level of the *sangsāric* existence has been decided by the inclination of desire, a certain type of desire will choose a kind of body-form in that level of existence. In other words, within the level of existence there are many different manifestations. For example, in the level of the animal world there are many kinds of animals. As soon as the dead has entered into the animal world, he chooses a certain kind of body-form according to the types of desire he has. For example, if he has a desire for sensuality, he will be attracted to the dog-form. If the desire of selfishness and uncleanliness dominates him, he may be attracted by the pig-form. If he has the lust for worldly possessions and industry, he may be attracted by the ant-form. It is also possible that the dead may seek the tiger-form if his desire corresponds to the character of the tiger. Therefore, whatever the dead desires, he will seek after. Since his desire to seek after comes from the basic inclination to act in a certain way, the choice of the body-form in the process of reincarnation is also dependent on *karma*.

If the choice of the womb-door is dependent on the kind of *karma* the dead possesses, how can the *Bardo* body or astral body be changed to the sub-human form of body? According to the *Bardo Thödol*, the *Bardo* body, which is also the mode of the *karma* complex, may likely retain itself without too much change for a certain period of time after death. However, the complex can be completely dissolved and disintegrated into the sub-human forms on different atoms and enter into the inorganic kingdoms if the after-death state is unduly prolonged. Thus the longer the dead continues his *Bardo* journey, the less possibility he has of retaining the original level of existence. That is why the *Bardo Thödol* teaches that the most favorable moment of liberation is the very moment of death. The decreasing intensity of lights in the second and third *Bardo* periods indicates the degeneration of the genetic and mental complex. Evans-Wentz seems to summarize the very essence of what I have attempted to say in this regard:

The esoteric teaching concerning this may be stated literally: That which is common to the human and to the sub-human worlds alike, namely matter in its varied aspects as solids, liquids, and gases, eternally transmigrates. That which is specifically human and specifically sub-human remains so, in accordance with the law of nature that like attracts like and produces like, that all forces ever follow the line of least resistance, that such highly evolved mental compounds as are bound up with the complex human consciousness cannot be disintegrated instantaneously, but require due allowance of time for their degeneration and ultimate dissolution and transmigration. [19]

The idea of the transmigration of the human to the sub-human is based on the idea that the mental complex or the consciousness-complex can retrograde into a lower state of consciousness. Without the retrogression of the conscious complex, the reincarnation of the human into the sub-human being is not possible. However, individual *karma* seems not to alter its direction. There is a close relationship between individual *karma* and the complex of DNA (deoxyribonucleic acid) and RNA (ribonucleic acid) in contemporary biological science. In other words, if *karma* is the basis of psychic heredity, we can safely say that *karma* is the background of the genetic code of the DNA-RNA complex. Since this genetic code is universal in all the living beings, *karma* is universal. Thus we see the continuity among all the living. According to the *I Ching*, there are 64 germinal situations which are the sums of all possible types in the world. However, it seems more than mere coincidence that George Gamow's 64 possible genetic-code combinations are strikingly similar to the 64 types of *karma*, expressed in the germinal situations of the *I Ching*.

If we follow the hypothesis that individual *karma* is the foundation of the DNA complex, we can explain the process of transformation from the spiritual body (or the *Bardo* body) to the physical body more reasonably to our contemporary mind. The nature of reincarnation deals with the process of transformation from the invisible to the visible manifestation. The *Bardo Thödol* describes this process of transformation as the method of closing the womb-door. In this process, the power of *karma* seems to have the means to bring both sexes together in the act of procreation. It is, then, the *karma* as the foundation of the genetic code or DNA molecules that brings about the union of the sperm and the ovum. Thus the kind of genetic code that man possesses is possible because of *karma*. Since the *Bardo* body is none other than the consciousness of the *karmic* complex, the transformation of this body to the living is none other than the activation of the DNA complex, which seems to fabricate new cellular protein. The *Bardo Thödol* uses symbolic language to describe the transformation.

[when] entering upon the path of ether, just at the moment when the sperm and the ovum are about to unite — the Knower experienceth the bliss of the simultaneously-born state, during which state it fainteth away into unconsciousness. [Afterwards] it findeth itself encased in oval form, in the embryonic state, and upon emerging from the womb and opening its eyes it may find itself transformed into a young dog. [20]

From the above descriptions we see the consciousness-complex of *karma* is to be understood as the basis of the genetic code. Thus *karma* is the spiritual power of renewal of the dead. Through it, the dead receive life.

It is rather amazing that the view of the Freudian psychoanalyst is remarkably supported in the *Bardo Thòdol*. The Freudian doctrine of the aversion of the son for the father is clearly expressed in the process of rebirth. The passage in the *Sidpa Bardo* says:

If [about] to be born as a male, the feeling of itself being a male dawneth upon the Knower, and a feeling of intense hatred towards the father and of jealousy and attraction towards the mother is begotten. If [about] to be born as a female, the feeling of itself being a female dawneth upon the Knower, and a feeling of intense hatred towards the mother and of intense attraction and fondness towards the father is begotten. [21]

As it has been indicated here, the sexual fantasies of repulsion and attachment have been known even to the fetus. Thus, Carl Jung reports that

psychoanalysts even claim to have proved back to memories of intra-uterine origin.

He thinks that

Freudian psychoanalysis could have happily pursued these so-called intra-uterine experiences still further back; had it succeeded in this bold undertaking, it would surely have come out beyond the *Sidpa Bardo* and penetrated from behind into the lower reaches of the *Chönyid Bardo*. [22]

The Western psychoanalysts could not pursue further than the experience of the *Sidpa Bardo*, because the existing biological ideas are not fully equipped with a kind of philosophy to experiment in the non-biological sphere.

Therefore, Edward B. Tylor, one of the great anthropologists of modern time, remarked that the doctrine of reincarnation is more reasonable than any other claim. He said,

So it may seem that the original idea of transmigration was the straightforward and reasonable one of human souls being reborn in new human bodies . . . The beast is the very incarnation of familiar qualities of man; and such names as lion, bear, fox, owl, parrot, viper, worm, when we apply them as epithets to men condense into a word some leading feature of human life.[23]

Through the process of reincarnation the dead is brought to the counterpole of death. When the existence of self is seen in terms of the whole, both dead and birth are complementary to each other. Birth is the other pole of death and death is the other side of birth. Thus, we can say, as Lāma Anagarika Govinda said,

There is not *one* person, indeed, not *one* living being, that has *not* returned from death. Infact, we all have died many deaths, before we came into this incarnation. And what we call birth is merely the reverse side of death, like one of the two sides of a coin, or like a door which we call "entrance" from outside and "exit" from inside a room.[24]

Everything, including the human being, is subject to the principle of changes, which operates through the power of cyclic recurrence. The essential structure of the whole universe may not alter because of changes, but one may alter from one archetype to another archetype through the recurrences of death and birth. Both the living and death experiences are inseparably related to each other. Death is a passive side of life, and life is the active side of death. What is experienced in life is to be fulfilled and completed in death. Thus the death experience is the reversal of the life experience. Just as yin is the reverse of yang, death is the other side of life. In this kind of complementary relationship, the process of reincarnation is none other than part of a changing process. Thus reincarnation is the process of renewal and evolvement.

In the process of reincarnation the spiritual body, which is the karmically inclined aggregate of energies, begins to manifest itself in the form of the physical body; whereas, in the process of death the physical body changes to the spiritual or the *Bardo* body. Neither is death the process of extinction, nor is birth the process of creation. Nothing is eliminated or added to the wholeness of the universe. Every form of change is none other than the process of transition within the opposite poles. Thus, the doctrine of reincarnation, just like the law of conservation of energy, is based on conservation of psychic or spiritual energy, which presupposes the wholeness of the universe. In the micro- and macrocosmic view of the world, human existence represents the quantum of the universe. The human body as the quantum of the universal body may have to adhere to the process of transition within the poles of birth and death. Within these two opposite poles the spiritual body can transform itself to the physical body, just as energy is changed to mass. Thus the process of reincarnation, that is, the process of transformation from the spiritual to the physical body, is reasonable to the concept of life and death in Eastern perspective.

NOTES AND REFERENCES

[1] His article "Is There Another Life After Death? A Scientist Investigates Claims of Reincarnation and Finds Phenomena not Explained by Ordinary Laws of Nature," in Oct. 2, 1970 issue, pp. 84ff.

[2] His *Life Begins At Death* (Nashville: Abingdon Press, 1969), p. 72.

[3] *Ibid.*, p. 71.

[4] The principle of changes is based on the expansion and contraction of yin and yang. Thus it moves in the form of a circle. See J. Y. Lee, *The Principle of Changes*, pp. 53ff.

[5] See J. Y. Lee, "The *I Ching* and Modern Science," delivered at 28th International Congress of Orientalists in Canberra, Australia, Jan., 1971.

[6] Rudolf Bultmann, "New Testament and Mythology," in *Kerygma and Myth: A Theological Debate*, Ed. by Hans Werner Bartsch, Trans. by Reginald H. Fuller (London: S.P.C.K., 1957), p. 1.

[7] *Katha Upanishad*, I.6.

[8] II Macc. 7:22f.

[9] *The Tibetan Book of the Dead*, Ed. by W. Y. Evans-Wentz (New York: Oxford University Press, 1957), pp. 164-165.

[10] *The Tibetan Book of the Dead*, p. 161.

[11] *Ibid.*, p. 166.

[12] *The Tibetan Book of the Dead*, p. 173.

[13] *Ibid.*, p. 174.

[14] *Ibid.*

[15] Sarvepalli Radharkrishnan, *The Hindu View of Life* (New York: The Macmillan Company, 1931), p. 52.

[16] Carl Jung, "Psychological Commentary," in *The Tibetan Book of the Dead*, p. xliii.

[17] *The Tibetan Book of the Dead*, pp. 60-61.

[18] The 64 hexagrams in the *I Ching* represent to all the possible phenomena of the universe. They symbolize the germinal situations or archetypes which are manifested in the myriads of different things. For full explanation see J. Y. Lee, *The Principle of Changes*, pp. 129ff.

[19] *The Tibetan Book of the Dead*, pp. 46-47.

[20] *The Tibetan Book of the Dead*, p. 179.

[21] *Ibid.*, p. 179.

[22] Carl Jung, "Psychological Commentary," in *The Tibetan Book of the Dead*, pp. xli-xlii.

[23] Edwards B. Tylor, *Primitive Culture* (London, 1891), ii. 17.

[24] Lama Anagarika Govinda, "Introductory Foreword" in *The Tibetan Book of the Dead*, p. lii.

9 | *Overcoming the Power of Death*

There is no way to overcome the power of death unless we recognize death in relation to life. Death can control us when we are ignorant about it. Death itself does not possess the power to rule over us, but we often attribute to it the power over us because of our ignorance. Our ignorance means to make death the enemy of life. When death becomes the enemy of life, death gets the power to control us. We all know that we must die. If death is the enemy of life, our life has to surrender its power to death when we die. Death then becomes the lord of life, because every living being is destined to die. If we put all our values in life alone, death takes away everything we have. That is why our ignorance of death in relation to life makes death all-powerful.

As we said, death is not an enemy of life but a counterpart of life. Death belongs to the realm of yin, life to the realm of yang. Just as yin and yang are not enemies to each other, death and life are not in conflict. Just as yin and yang are complementary to each other for the rounded whole, death is necessary for the completion of life and life necessitates death for its renewal. Just as darkness is possible because of light and light because of darkness, death is possible because of life and life because of death. This mutual inclusiveness and interdependence makes it possible for us to overcome the power of death. If we are ignorant about this complementary relationship between life and death, we cannot overcome the power of death. That is why the first step of our overcoming the power of death deals with the right understanding of death in relation to life.

When we fail to understand this complementary relationship between death and life, we become the victims of the fear of death. When we are afraid of death, we become the victims of this fear. We are afraid of the fear of death, rather than death itself. Thus, as Carl Jung indicates, most emotional problems of those over forty are one way or another due to the fear of death. When we are afraid of our own fear, we accumulate another fear over the existing fear of our own. In this way our fear is constantly intensified and becomes beyond our control. When we are no longer capable of

90

controlling ourselves over the fear of our own fear, we become the slaves of death. To be the slave of death means, then, to become the slave of our own illusion, because we become the servants of that which we have created in our mind. When we become the servants of death, that is, the servants of our own illusion, we are desperate for life. But life also rejects us, for it is in death. In other words, we want to cling to life, but life gradually breaks us loose into the abyss of death. That is why those who are afraid of the fear of death are the most tragic figures in the world. We cannot escape that fear unless we understand that death is a part of life. When we come to know this inclusive relationship between them, we do not have to cling to life alone. To rely on life means also to depend on death, for both life and death are inseparably related to each other. Thus, to overcome the power of death means to understand this inseparable relationship between death and life. When we have overcome the power of death, we are no longer the object of that power. We become the subject of death. We control the power of death, which becomes our object. To be the subject of death means then to overcome the power of death. However, we cannot be the subjects of death unless we are the subjects of life. That is precisely why those who have overcome life can also overcome death. On the other hand, those who are afraid of death cannot live life without fear. It is then those who know how to live who will know how to die also. At the same time, those who are willing to face death will live their life in peace. Thus, *The Book of the Craft of Dying* said,

Learn to die and thou shalt learn to live, for there shall none learn to live that hath not learned to die. [1]

Since death and life are inseparably interrelated, there is no way to prevent one from dying. To stop the process of death is in fact to stop living. Not to die means not to live altogether. That is why the way of overcoming the power of death is not to stop the reality of death, but to prevent the possibility of the recurrence of death. In other words, to control the power of death means to prevent the recurrence of death and birth. Since death is inevitable for those who have life, the prevention of death is also the prevention of life. Thus to stop the recurrence of death means to stop the process of birth for life. The prevention of death is then the prevention of birth also. Not to be born again means not to die again. Thus birth control is in fact death control.

If the most effective means of preventing the recurrence of death is the prevention of birth, we must find a way to stop the dead from reincarnation. If we do not believe in the idea of reincarnation, the recurrence of death can be prevented by the contemporary method of birth control through the use of medical technology. However, if we seriously believe in the reality of reincarnation, we must consider the serious consequence that can be produced by the artificial means of birth control in our time. Since the idea of reincarnation presupposes the survival of the dead, the artificial means of birth prevention in our time may cause the dead to seek an undesirable body for rebirth or to wander around in the *Bardo* world without finding the womb-door to enter in. According to the *Bardo Thödol*, the *Bardo* body or the aggregate of energies gradually disintegrates itself when the normal process of reincarnation is unduly prolonged. Thus the use of birth control through medical technology in our time may not be an effective means to overcome the power of death. The most effective method of overcoming the recurrence of death and birth is known as liberation.

Liberation is the ultimate means of overcoming the power of death. It is freedom from the chain of birth and death. It is a means of extinguishing the desire or inclination to possess the *sangsāric* body. The desire to be born again in the *sangsāric* world comes from the *karmic* illusion of the dead. Thus liberation is also known as the cessation of *karma*. When *karma* is no longer powerful to dominate the mentality of the *Bardo* body, he is liberated from the power of death. Death possesses power only when the dead is in illusion or in ignorance. When the dead is liberated from this illusion, he is aware of the Clear Light of the Void, which is the radiance of his true Self, the archetype of Cosmic consciousness. Thus liberation is the realization of his real Self. By realizing his true Self he is no longer the slave of his unreal self, which is expressed in the *karmic* visions and hallucinations. Liberation is then the realization of one's true Self, which is the inmost essence of his existence. Through the realization of true Self one may be freed from the illusory visions of fear. When the true Self is realized, he is no longer an object of change. He becomes the subject of everything that changes. Thus to be the true Self means to be the change-itself in the world of change and transformation. He becomes the axis of a moving wheel. He is no longer subject to the power of change, because he is a part of that change that changes the world. To be the change-itself, the source of changes, in the world of change is to be the Tao or the Absolute, which is subject of the changing process through the cycle of birth and death. When he becomes the subject of this changing process, he has overcome the power of death and rebirth.

How can the dying or the dead obtain liberation? Does he have to do it by himself? Is there anyone who can assist him to obtain this liberation? The *Bardo Thödol* makes it clear that the dying person or the dead is the captain of his own soul. He is primarily responsible for his own destiny and his own liberation from the chain of birth and death. What he *is* will decide what he will become. According to *Karma* or the law of cause and effect, one's destiny is conditioned by his past. His life is the cause which will affect him in death. That is why it is often said that life is the stage of preparation for death. Since death is the reverse process of life, what is recorded in the movie film of life will be replayed in an inverse order in death. Thus what he has been in life will condition the life after death. If we illustrate it again through the use of the same metaphor of a diver, we may be able to see the clear relationship between life and death in the attainment of liberation. If the goal of the diver is to take hold of a rock under the water, he must do his best to prepare the deepest dive he can make. In order to do it, he has to accumulate enough power to project himself from the diving board. The greater the projection he can make from the diving board, the deeper the layer of water he can reach. In other words, what he does on the diving board, which is analogous with life, will effect how deep he can dive into the water. Just as the last moment of his preparation at the diving board is most important in his diving efficiency, the last moment of the dying process is the dominating factor of the dead in attaining the eternal liberation from the chain of birth and death. The disposition of this last moment is often called the last thought. As Gunaratna said,

This last thought series is most important since it fashions the nature of his next existence, just as the last thought before going to sleep can become the first thought on awakening. [2]

Just as the diver puts all the effort he has made to the very moment of diving himself off from the board, the dying person brings everything that is of himself to the very moment of death. Thus, the *Bardo Thödol* describes that the greatest possible moment of liberation is the *Chikhai Bardo*, which means the dying moment. Just as the diver can reach the deepest abyss of water as soon as he has made a dive, the dying person can reach the deepest layer of unconsciousness when he is in the very moment of "swoon". If the diver can reach deep enough to take hold of the rock, he does not have to return to the surface of the water. Likewise, the dead person does not have to return to the world if he is united with the deepest layer of unconsciousness, the true Self or the Cosmic Unconsciousness. To reach that deepest part of his own nature one must do everything he can in life. Thus life prepares him for the ultimate liberation from the recurrence of death and birth.

Even though each individual is responsible for his own destiny, he is not without the assistance of others. The *Bardo Thödol* seems to suggest that the dying person can be assisted by his priests or gurus through the reading of sacred texts. The very title of the *Bardo Thödol*, which means "the art of liberation by hearing on the after-death plane," suggests the way of influencing the mental condition of the dying person through the reading of this book. It is a common practice of almost all religions to read the sacred texts and pray to the dying or the dead in order to assist him in this critical moment of transition. One of the most important functions of reading the sacred scripture or prayer is to help the dying person obtain the good terminal thought. [3] We hear the constant repetition of the sacred name, Mary the Mother of Jesus, at the funeral service of a Catholic Christian. Many

Protestant Christians do not chant the sacred names or the sacred texts, but they offer prayers and meditations for the dead. Almost all religions attempt to provide a kind of situation in which the dying person may obtain a good terminal thought. The very essence of the *Bardo Thödol* is to assist the dying or the dead not only for the formation of a good terminal thought but for the ultimate liberation from the power of *karma*. As soon as the diagnosis of death symptons is about to be completed, the spiritual leader begins to read the sacred instructions to the dying person. In order to condition the mind of the dying person, the reader puts his lips close to the ear and repeats the instructions clearly and distinctly. As the text says,

In saying this, the reader shall put his lips close to the ear, and shall repeat it distinctly, clearly impressing it upon the dying person so as to prevent his mind from wandering even for a moment. [4]

In order to give the firm impression of the final thought to the dying person, the reader can repeat the instructions three or even seven times a day. [5] The instructions which the guru reads to the dying person deal with more than the formation of a good terminal thought. They actually instruct the dying person as to what he can do to liberate himself from the *karmic* illusions which are about to appear to him. Without the repeated instruction of the guru to the dying person it is difficult for him to recognize the Clear Light of the Void for liberation. Even though he may be familiar with the instructions in life, he may not be able to recognize the Clear Light of the Void because of his serious mental disruptions by the disease. As the text says,

There may be even those who have made themselves familiar with the teachings, yet who, because of the violence of the disease causing death, may be mentally unable to withstand illusions. For such, also, this instruction is absolutely necessary. [6]

Thus the *Bardo Thödol* stresses the importance of instruction to the dying person to attain liberation. Without this instruction the dying person may not be able to focus his mentality on the radiance of his true Self, which appears as the Clear Light.

It is reasonable to believe that the dying person can be benefited by the instructions of the guru, but it is questionable to continue the same kind of instructions to the dead for the forty-nine days of the *Bardo* journey. How can the dead hear the instruction of the guru? If the dead is unable to hear the instruction, it seems a waste of time to repeat the sacred texts after death. This is perhaps why most Christians direct their prayers to God rather than to the dead. However, according to the *Bardo Thödol*, the instructions are directed to the dead, since liberation is ultimately dependent on his recognition of the Clear Light. We see the reason why the instructions are given to the dead. The dead, according to the *Bardo Thödol*, can hear the readings of the guru. That is, the dead is conscious and the guru can mediate his voice to him.

There is a growing interest in the West in the possibility of the survival of the dead and the possible communication with them. Even though the majority of contemporary scientists assert that consciousness must cease with the death of the body, there are others who do not want to close the door on the possibility of the survival of the consciousness of the dead. For example, Erwin Schroedinger believes that the conscious is inextinguishable:

In no case is there a loss of personal consciousness to deplore. Nor will there ever be. [7]

One of the sensational stories in our times was made by James A. Pike, Episcopal Bishop, who convincingly testifies his experience of communication with his dead son through spiritual mediums. [8] Even though parapsychology made some progress in the area of para-normal phenomena which deal with the non-empirical world, it is still in an experimental stage. If what Carl Jung has said is right, the East is far ahead in psychic study. He said,

We Westerners, in spite of our so-called culture, are still barbarians and children when it comes to the psychic world. We have only just rediscovered the precious stone; we have still to polish it. We cannot yet compete with the intuitive clarity of Eastern vision. [9]

Moreover, if we believe that the *Bardo Thödol* is the most authentic account of death from the East, [10] it is possible that what is said in this book can be very significant to our understanding of the spiritual world.

According to the *Bardo Thödol*, the consciousness-principle is retained even after death. In the second stage of the *Bardo* period, that is, in the *Chönyid Bardo*, the consciousness will take up the ethereal body. Thus the text says,

While on the second stage of the *Bardo*, one's body is of the nature of that called the shining illusory-body. [11]

Because the consciousness-principle is retained in the ethereal body, the dead can visualize the various visions and hear the different sounds during his *Bardo* journey. Even though the dead is conscious, there is no way for an ordinary person to communicate with him. The guru then acts as a spiritual medium to the dead. Since he can communicate with the dead, he can instruct the dead what to do to liberate himself from the power of *karma*. The idea of communication with the dead is based on the law of energy vibration. Each archetype of energies seems to possess its own rate of vibration. To know the rate of this vibration for the dead is a key to the understanding of telepathic communication with the dead. The gurus are the guardians of the secret insight. Knowing this secret insight, the guru can correlate the particular rate of vibration of the physical forces with that of the spiritual beings. The correlation of these dissimilar vibrations is a task of the spiritual leader in order to guide the dead on the safe journey of the *Bardo*, as well as for the final liberation from the world of death and birth.

Let us, then, conclude what we have attempted to say in regard to the overcoming of death. What the *Bardo Thödol* teaches us is primarily the process of self-control and self-realization at death. It helps us to overcome the false power based on the illusions and ignorance of our own creation. To overcome this false power which we have objectified is in fact to overcome the power of death. Death does not have the power in itself but is given the power because of our fear of it. Through the elimination of this false power we will be freed from the cycle of birth and death. We do not remain subject to the cycle, because we become the essence or subject of this cyclic change. Being freed means to become the essence of change, that is, to be one with the true Self, the Cosmic Mind or the Ultimate ground of all existence. To become a part of that Ultimate is to overcome the power of death forever. That is, then, the ultimate goal of all the living and the dead.

NOTES AND REFERENCES

[1] *The Tibetan Book of the Dead*, p. iv.

[2] V. F. Gunaratna, *Buddhist Reflections on Death* (Kandy, Ceylon: Buddhist Publication Society, 1966), p. 33.

[3] *Ibid.*

[4] *The Tibetan Book of the Dead*, p. 95.

[5] *Ibid.*, p. 97.

[6] *The Tibetan Book of the Dead*, p. 100.

[7] Erwin Schroedinger, *What is Life?* (Cambridge University Press, 1951), p. 92.

[8] See James A. Pike, *The Other Side: My Experience with Psychic Phenomena* (New York: Doubleday, 1968).

[9] Carl G. Jung, *The Integration of the Personality*, Trans. by Stanley Dell (London: Kegan Paul, Trench, Trubmer, 1940), p. 41.

[10] Saher, *op. cit.*, p. 248.

[11] *The Tibetan Book of the Dead*, p. 100.

INDEX